GRACED MOMENTS

Prayer Services for the Lives of Teens

Therese Brown

VOLUME ONE

WORLD LIBRARY PUBLICATIONS
3825 North Willow Road
Schiller Park, Illinois 60176

Copyright © 2001, World Library Publications.
3825 N. Willow Road, Schiller Park, Illinois 60176
All rights reserved.

ISBN 1-58459-075-0

Excerpts from the *Consistent Ethic of Life* by Joseph Cardinal Bernardin are reprinted with permission of the Archdiocese of Chicago. All rights reserved.

No part of this book may be reproduced or transmitted in any form or by any means, including reproduction by mechanical, photographic or electronic means, without written permission from the copyright holder.

This book was edited by Jerry Galipeau. The copy editor was Marcia T. Lucey and the design is by Kathy Ade and Tejal Patel.

Music suggestions for the prayer services are drawn from WLP's popular contemporary hymnal, *Voices as One*. The hymnal, four-CD set, and accompaniments for keyboard and guitar are available by calling WLP Customer Care at 800 566-6150, or by visiting our web site at wlpmusic.com.

Hymnal	006591
Four CDs	006594
Keyboard Accompaniment	006590
Guitar Accompaniment	006597

Printed in the United States of America

CONTENTS

THE CALENDAR YEAR
    Advent 6
    Christmas 8
    Martin Luther King, Jr. 10
    Pro-life Month 12
    Lent..15
    Easter 18
    Feasts of the Saints & Name Days 20

YOUTH PILGRIMAGES
    Blessings for Departure and Return of Pilgrims 22

ATHLETICS
    Start of Athletic Season 25
    Start of an Athletic Game..27

SCHOOL CALENDAR AND ACTIVITIES
    Beginning of the School Year 28
    Prayer before Homecoming or Prom 31
    Prayer before Exams 33
    Blessing of Graduates 36
    Baccalaureate 38
    Prayer in Time of Stress 40

LEADERSHIP
    Commissioning of Leaders 42

CONTENTS

YOUTH MEDIA
Youth Movies 45
Youth Music 47
Youth Videos 49

SACRAMENTAL PREPARATION
Commitment to Preparation Process for Confirmation 51

DEATH
Death of a Classmate..54

DRIVING
Blessing of Driver's Licenses and Keys 56

INITIATION
Entering the Initiation Process..58

FORGIVENESS
Forgiveness..61

CHRISTIAN SERVICE
Blessing of Objects Used in Service Projects 63
Blessing of Hands for Christian Service..65

VIOLENCE
Violence Within the Local Community 67
Violence Outside the Local Community 69

DEDICATION

To the young women of Resurrection High School, Chicago, Illinois, to the teens of St. John the Evangelist, Columbia, Maryland, to Andy and every young person who was touched or touched a life during the National Catholic Youth Conference, to the adults who coordinate youth ministry programs, and to Tony.

ADVENT Advent

MATERIALS NEEDED

8.5 x 11 inch paper (construction, white)
Pencils, pens, or markers
Scissors
Newsprint or chalkboard (optional)

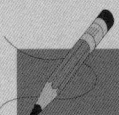
NOTES

- During this prayer service, the participants will use cut-outs of their feet. If time does not allow it, cut out pairs of feet for each participant beforehand.
- To prepare the space, remove all chairs and tables, and divide the floor area into three parallel sections using tape, a line of books, rows of candles—whatever objects you have available and feel comfortable using. At the beginning of the service, the participants will sit in one of the end sections, then move to the center section for the majority of the service. Make sure that the center section is big enough (wide and long) to accommodate all of the expected participants—they should be a little crowded!
- Invite the participants to sit in one of the end sections as they arrive. Leave the other end section blank throughout the service.

GATHERING

- As a part of the gathering, share some brief instructions on this short activity with the participants.
- Pass out one sheet of paper and a pencil, pen, or marker to each person.
- Invite each participant to trace the outline of their feet on the paper, then cut out the tracings.
- In the background, play quiet, reflective music.
- When the participants have completed the cut-outs, ask them to write their responses to the statement below on both of the cut-out feet. They can list as many responses as they would like. Feel free to post the statement on newsprint or a chalkboard, if one is available.
- When they are finished listing their responses, ask them to set their cut-out feet on the ground, facing the center section, then to move and sit in the center section.

As baptized Christians, we have committed ourselves to imitating Jesus in our daily lives—to loving our neighbors and ourselves, to forgiving each other, to helping those in need.

Name some of the ways in which you have acted or spoken during the past year as Jesus might have.

Leader: In the name of the Father,
and of the Son,
and of the Holy Spirit.

All: Amen.

Leader: Let us pray.
God of the unexpected,
you promised us a Savior,
a Redeemer to deliver us from oppression.
In Jesus, you challenged our expectations.

You did not send a great king.
You gave us a carpenter's son
who spoke words of kindness and love,
and performed acts of compassion
   and forgiveness
among the least important of the world.
Then, most unexpectedly, he asked us
   to do the same.
As we wait this Advent,
open our hearts to your unexpected Word,
so that we might continue his work
and free our world from oppression.
We ask this through Christ our Lord.

All: Amen.

Reading: Luke 3:10–18

REFLECTION

Invite the young people to share some of the experiences that they listed on the cut-out feet in small groups or in the large group.

Ask them the following questions:

1. Why do you believe that your actions or words imitated what Jesus might have done?
2. Which actions or words were easy? Which ones were difficult? Why?

TALKING POINTS

As you break open the Word, some points to share include:

- This Gospel is the reading for the Third Sunday of Advent in Year C. With the Third Sunday of Advent, we make a transition from readings that focus on preparing for Jesus' second coming to readings that focus on his first coming.
- It is important to note that during this change in focus, we continue to be called to do the same things in preparation for the second coming as for the first coming of the Messiah. We are called to repent, to do justice, to live righteously, to be peaceful.
- There are two key phrases in this passage: "What then shall we do?" and "As the people were in expectation . . ."
- Many of those who gathered around John the Baptist in this reading were probably Jews, anxious to find out if John was the Messiah.
- They were in expectation, waiting for their Messiah, living their lives in preparation for that day. What they found and what they were asked to do was not exactly what they expected.
- For example, tax collectors and soldiers used their positions to take more than what they were owed from others and they were asked to change.
- This Advent reading sets the stage for all of Jesus' preaching. Jesus will continue to ask his followers to take the unexpected action if they want to follow him.
- Jesus expects that we continue to take these actions to build up the Kingdom as we wait for his coming again at the end of time.

REFLECTION QUESTIONS

The following reflection questions can be considered in small groups (duos or triads), then shared with the large group.

1. If I were to ask John the question, "What then shall I do?" what unexpected action might he tell me to do to prepare for the coming of Jesus during this Advent? (Hint: For certain young people, missing a practice or an athletic game to stay home with family might be an example.)
2. How might this action help me prepare myself better to receive Jesus in my life?
3. What support do I need from the people here to help me do as John might tell me?
4. What do I need from God to help me take this action?

Intercessions

Invite the young people to ask God out loud for what they need in order to take the unexpected action as the intercessions for this service.

Response: Lord, hear our prayer.

CLOSING

Our Father…

Suggested songs include:

On That Holy Mountain (Mattingly)
   Voices as One Hymnal #68, CD 3 Track 14

Strength for the Journey (Poirier)
   Voices as One Hymnal #87, CD 4 Track 8

We Are the Hope (Tate)
   Voices as One Hymnal #97, CD 4 Track 17

Look to the One (Bolduc)
   Voices as One Hymnal #57, CD 3 Track 5

Christmas

MATERIALS NEEDED

Empty boxes or envelopes
   (one for each participant)
Heavy paper
   (construction paper, special printing paper)
Markers, pens
Wrapping paper
Ribbon

NOTES

- This prayer service can be done toward the end of Advent or, preferably, during the Christmas season, up through the feast of the Baptism of the Lord. The closing prayer will need to be modified if the service is held during Advent.
- Set the prayer space in an appropriately festive way.
- Suggestions:
  - Decorate large pieces of paper or poster board with quotes from the Gospels, highlighting each of the main characters that appear throughout the Christmas readings—Mary, Joseph, the Magi, the shepherds, King Herod, Simeon, Anna, and the disciples. Place them around the space and invite the young people to read them as they gather.
  Play instrumental music in the background.
  - Place brightly wrapped boxes (even empty ones) around a large lit candle at the center of the space to focus on the relationship between the experience of presents and presence.

GATHERING

Leader: In the name of the Father,
and of the Son,
and of the Holy Spirit.

All: Amen.

Call to Worship: Colossians 3:15b–16

Leader:

Paul invites us to give God thanks with psalms and hymns and inspired songs.

In this Christmas season of thankfulness and praise, let us sing together _____.

Select a well-known Christmas song or carol that expresses joy and gratitude to sing after the Call to Worship.

Reading: Colossians 3:12–17

TALKING POINTS

As you break open the Word, some points to share include:

- Christmas focuses on the incarnate presence of God in Jesus—God made flesh who lived among us.
- While we tend to focus on Jesus as the main character of the infancy narratives and the Gospels up through his baptism, the Gospels also break open the stories of those who recognized God's presence in Jesus—Mary, Joseph, the Magi, the shepherds, Simeon, Anna, and the disciples—and how they responded.
- Those who believed that Jesus was the Messiah gave God thanks and glorified him.
- Like those in the infancy narratives, Paul reminds the Colossians and us that we must give thanks to God in everything that we do.
- Paul also gives the Colossians and us a list of attitudes and behaviors that we must "put on" in order to continue to make Jesus present to others.

REFLECTION QUESTIONS

1. To whom do you need to be more present at this time of year?
2. What gift of yourself do you need to share with that person?
3. How will you be more present to that person?

RITUAL

- Using the answer to the third reflection question, create a certificate with the available paper, redeemable by the person you identified in your reflection.
- Include an expiration date of no later than January 15—about the end of the Christmas season.
- Decorate the certificate and wrap it in the envelope or box.
- Deliver it to the person during the Christmas season.

Variation

Focus this reflection on the needs of the larger community (parish, school, neighborhood).

Identify groups of people for whom the youth need to be more present.

Invite participants to create certificates, redeemable by the parish/school leader, for a certain number of hours or a certain activity that would help them be more present to the community. Examples include hours at a senior home, hours tutoring younger students, walking in the next hunger walk, cooking dinner at the homeless shelter.

CLOSING

Leader: After each phrase, please respond "We thank you, God."

> For compassion and kindness . . .
> For lowliness and meekness . . .
> For patience and forbearance . . .
> For forgiveness and love . . .
> For peace and unity . . .
> For your Son, Jesus Christ . . .
> For tongues to sing . . .
> For voices to shout . . .

Suggested closing song:

A Christmas carol like *Joy to the World*.

M.L. King, Jr.

MATERIALS NEEDED

Lengths of ribbon, common string, heavy rope, and light wire

Can of Silly String™

Slips of paper or index cards

NOTES

- During Part Two of the reflection, have the participants write their answers on slips of paper or index cards in preparation for the closing prayer.

GATHERING

Suggested songs include:

All Will Be Well (Warner)
  Voices as One Hymnal #1, CD 1 Track 1

By the Waters of Babylon (Tate)
  Voices as One Hymnal #13, CD 1 Track 11

Leader:	In the name of the Father, and of the Son, and of the Holy Spirit.
All:	Amen.
Reading:	Isaiah 61:1–3

REFLECTION ACTIVITY

Part One

Divide the group into five small groups.

- Tie each group up with one of the five materials. The group may be tied up in multiple ways: standing with one long length bound around them like stalks of wheat; wound around each of their wrists or ankles with the ends tied together to form a chain. Be creative and make this a challenge for the young people.

- Without untying any knots, give the groups a few minutes to try to free themselves from what binds them. They may not seek help from anyone else. After a few minutes, release everyone and lay out the used materials in the center of the prayer space where everyone can see them.

10

Ask each group to reflect on the following questions concerning their length of Silly String™, ribbon, string, rope, or wire; then share them with the whole group.

1. At the beginning of this activity, when you were first bound together, how did the members of your group feel about being bound?
2. What did it take to break the material that bound your group?

Read the Isaiah passage again.

TALKING POINTS

As you break open the Word and this activity, some points to share include:

- The people for whom Isaiah was writing hungered for these words of hope and freedom because they were prisoners in Babylon.
- This is the reading that Jesus quotes early in his ministry in the Gospel of Luke, telling those in the synagogue that these words are fulfilled in their midst.
- Throughout his ministry, Jesus speaks and acts in order to free people from whatever oppresses or afflicts them.
- Martin Luther King, Jr. had a vision of a world that was free from the kind of oppression that Isaiah's audience experienced, that Jesus' listeners knew, and that King's African American brothers and sisters lived on a daily basis.
- Jesus and King spent their lives trying to break people free of the bonds that held them captive.
- There are many "ropes" that prevent people from being free—"ism's", injustice—and they vary in strength like the materials we used.

REFLECTION ACTIVITY

Part Two

Ask each group to reflect on the following questions and share them with each other, then the large group. Their responses will be part of the closing prayer.

3. What experiences in our society are parallels for the strength of the material that bound you and prevented you from being free?
4. What can we do as a community to break those bonds in our society? What can you do as an individual?

CLOSING

Invite everyone to join hands in a circle.

> Remind them that the circle is a symbol of unity and our joined hands are a symbol of commitment to working together for freedom from whatever oppresses or afflicts people.

The closing prayer is a two-part litany.
The pattern for the litany follows.

Part One

Invite the participants to fill in the blank, "From _____" with their answers to question 3. For example, "From racism." The response is, "Free us, Lord."

Part Two

Invite the participants to fill in the blank, "For the courage to _____" with their answers to question 4.

For example, "For the courage to treat older people more kindly." The response is, "Lead us, Lord."

Suggested songs include:

I Have Been Anointed (Warner)
   Voices as One Hymnal #42, CD 2 Track 12

On a Journey Together (Angotti)
   Voices as One Hymnal #69, CD 3 Track 15

Show Us the Way (Light/Tate)
   Voices as One Hymnal #83, CD 4 Track 5

Pro-Life Month

MATERIALS NEEDED

One large sheet of white cloth that will be torn into strips 18 to 24 inches in length (enough for all participants)

Scissors

Variety of fabric paints (or markers)

Large cross (3 feet tall or more; not a crucifix)

NOTES

- The quoted passages are from two documents, *The Gospel of Life (Evangelium Vitae)* by Pope John Paul II and the *Consistent Ethic of Life* by Joseph Cardinal Bernardin.

- Anticipate discomfort with the issues that are named as a part of the image of the "seamless garment" and our Church's pro-life stance. Because of their political nature, the young people may have differing opinions on the individual issues. As much as possible, try to reconnect the individual issues with the larger image of one pro-life position.

- The strips of cloth used in the ritual activity are intended as symbols of the "seamed-ness," the torn nature of our society today (as opposed to the "seamlessness" of the pro-life position.)

- Place the cross in the center of the prayer space or at the front.

- Identify a place of reservation for the cross during the rest of the month to which the young people can return to pray.

GATHERING

As the young people gather, invite a few of them to tear the cloth into strips while the others assemble.

Music may be played in the background while people are gathering, or the young people might be led in an ostinato refrain.

Suggested song:

Be Holy (Bolduc)
   Voices as One Hymnal #8, CD 1 Track 7

Leader:	In the name of the Father, and of the Son, and of the Holy Spirit.
All:	Amen.

Readings

This set of readings has seven parts.

This is an opportunity to share the young people's gifts of proclamation by inviting several people to read.

Take a pause of about 20 to 30 seconds between each reading for reflection.

Reading 1:   Deuteronomy 30:15–16

Reading 2:   From *The Gospel of Life* by Pope John Paul II

Every human person is created in the image and likeness of God. The conviction that human life is sacred and that each person has inherent dignity that must be respected in society lies at the heart of Catholic social teaching. Calls to advance human rights are illusions if the right to life itself is subject to attack. We believe that every human life is sacred from conception to natural death; that people are more important than things; and that the measure of every institution is whether or not it enhances the life and dignity of the human person.

Reading 3: From the *Consistent Ethic of Life* by Joseph Cardinal Bernardin

The case for a consistent ethic of life—one which stands for the protection of the right to life and the promotion of the rights which enhance life from womb to tomb—manifests the positive potential of the Catholic moral and social tradition. … It is both a complex and a demanding tradition; it joins the humanity of the unborn infant and the humanity of the hungry; it calls for positive legal action to prevent the killing of the unborn or the aged and positive societal action to provide shelter for the homeless and education for the illiterate.

Reading 4: Deuteronomy 30:19–20

Reading 5: From *The Gospel of Life* by Pope John Paul II

As Scripture says, no house can stand divided against itself (Lk 11:17). We cannot simultaneously commit ourselves to human rights and progress while eliminating or marginalizing the weakest among us. Nor can we practice the Gospel of life only as a private piety. American Catholics must live it vigorously and publicly, as a matter of national leadership and witness, or we will not live it at all.

Reading 6: From the *Consistent Ethic of Life* by Joseph Cardinal Bernardin

Each of the issues I have identified today—abortion, war, hunger and human rights, euthanasia and capital punishment—is treated as a separate, self-contained topic in our public life. Each is distinct, but an ad hoc approach to each one fails to illustrate how our choices in one area can affect our decisions in other areas. There must be a public attitude of respect for all of life if public actions are to respect it in concrete cases.

Reading 7: Luke 10:25–37

TALKING POINTS

As you break open the Word, some points to share include:

- The choice that God presents to the Israelites in the desert—life or death—is the same choice that God presents to us today.
- Though the choice sounds simple, God's words make it clear that choosing life is anything but simple.
- Jesus picks up on the theme of the greatest commandment in the parable of the Good Samaritan, giving a stark example of how difficult it can be to choose life by loving God and our neighbor.
- Pope John Paul II reiterates Jesus' teaching that it is our responsibility to care for everyone just as the Good Samaritan cared for the injured man, and takes it one step further. Our responsibility is not only a private one—for our own individual choices—but a public responsibility to choose life for everyone in our society.
- Cardinal Bernardin brought together abortion, capital punishment, euthanasia, war, hunger, and homelessness as pro-life issues, connecting them through the image of the "seamless garment."
- The image of the "seamless garment" is a Gospel image, referring to the seamlessness or consistency of Jesus' preaching and living.

REFLECTION

Cardinal Bernardin names a number of "hot" issues—abortion, war, hunger, human rights, euthanasia, and capital punishment—as being part of the "big picture" of a consistent pro-life stance.

1. Before you came here, which ones would you name as being obviously pro-life issues? Why are they obvious? Which ones would you have left out? Why?

2. If we were to update the parable of the Good Samaritan so that the priest, the Levite, and the Samaritan encountered someone who was a victim of any of these "hot" issues, how would each of the three characters respond?

3. If choosing life means acting as though everyone we meet is sacred, who are the people in your daily life who are being treated as less than sacred? Who in your school? At work? In the community? In your city or town?

ACTIVITY & LITANY

Distribute the strips of cloth and fabric paint or markers to each person.

Invite them to write the name of someone or a group of people whose life we must nurture or support like the Good Samaritan did. Write on the end of the strip rather than the middle.

When they are finished writing, explain the prayer and litany.

> Each person is invited to come up to the cross and tie their strip of cloth on any part of the cross.
>
> As each person ties their piece of cloth, say "For" and the name of the person or people written on the cloth.
>
> Our response is, "Lord God, we choose life."

Leader (*after the litany*):

> Living God,
> you set the choice before us,
> life or death,
> and promised your eternal faithfulness
> to those who chose life.
> Today, we choose life for the unborn,
> for those struggling with chronic disease
>   and physical disabilities,
> for those who are abused
>   and those who are abusers;
> for the aged, the dying
>   and those awaiting execution,
> for the poor, the hungry, and the homeless,
> and for those ravaged by war.
> We ask for the strength to be faithful
>   to this choice,
> to be consistent with the whole of the
>   Gospel of Life
> who is Jesus.
> We ask for courage to use our voices publicly,
> to be witnesses among our friends and families
> and in our communities,
> to stand for life always.
> We ask this through Christ our Lord.

All: Amen.

CLOSING

Suggested songs include:

God's Love Is Eternal (Tate)
    Voices as One Hymnal #29, CD 2 Track 2

He Is Jesus (Bolduc)
    Voices as One Hymnal #34, CD 2 Track 6

Process the cross through the prayer space to its place of reservation—a chapel or the parish church, a special corner of a classroom.

Let the young people know that the cross will remain in this location throughout the month and encourage them to return to the cross to pray for those who face God's choice between life and death.

LENT
Ash Wednesday and the Season of Lent

 MATERIALS NEEDED

Small bowl with ashes

Paper or cloth towels (for the ashes and water)

Sand, rocks, cactus

Pictures of various people—saints, holy people, everyday people, children, the elderly, the dead, criminals

Large bowl with water and small drinking cups

Various candles, lanterns, or non-electric lamps—one for each participant, if possible

Palms or shrub branches

Cross or crucifix

Handmade or purchased journals (optional)

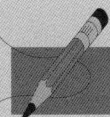 NOTES

- Though the readings are specifically chosen from Year A, the services can be done during any year. The readings allow the participants to reflect on the symbols of the season.
- This service is designed to be repeated once a week from Ash Wednesday through Holy Week. Various weeks can be compacted into fewer services by proclaiming the reading, doing the related ritual/reflection, then repeating the pattern for the next week.
- Each reflection question provides an opportunity to touch on our relationship with God, the community, and ourselves, and/or the corresponding three-fold practices of Lent: prayer, almsgiving, and fasting.
- Because these prayers can be used as a part of the Lenten practice of prayer, consider giving each participant a handmade or purchased journal to use for the reflections.
- Create an environment of stillness. Some suggested ways to do this are:
  - Dim the overhead lights.
  - Use no overhead light and only smaller lamps.

GATHERING

Leader: In the name of the Father,
and of the Son,
and of the Holy Spirit.

All: Amen.

Leader: Behold, now is the acceptable time;
behold, now is the day of salvation.

Let us pray.

> Gracious God,
> in this season of repentance,
> we the travelers on the way
>   to your Kingdom
> return to your loving embrace.
> May we walk in the warmth of your mercy
> as we journey to the coming Easter.
> We ask this through Christ our Lord.

All: Amen.

- Play soft solo instrumental music, or no music at all.
- Place signs or position hospitality ministers at the doors to the space to instruct the participants to enter in silence.
- Place the following in the center or at the front of the prayer space according to the week or readings chosen.
  - Ash Wednesday: Small bowl with ashes
  - 1st Sunday of Lent: Large bowl or pile of sand, rocks, cactus
  - 2nd Sunday of Lent: Pictures of various people
  - 3rd Sunday of Lent: Large bowl with water and small drinking cups
  - 4th Sunday of Lent: One large, lit candle with various other candles, lanterns, or non-electric lamps
  - Passion Sunday/Holy Week: Palms/shrub branches, crucifix or cross
- Host the prayer service in the parish/school chapel or church or a space other than that which is used for other youth activities.

Readings

Ash Wednesday:	2 Corinthians 5:20 — 6:2
1st Week of Lent:	Matthew 4:1–11
2nd Week of Lent:	Luke 9:28–36
3rd Week of Lent:	John 4:1–7
4th Week of Lent:	John 9:1–7
5th Week of Lent:	John 11:17–27
Holy Week:	Mark 11:8–10

RITUAL/REFLECTION

Ash Wednesday

Ritual:
Pass a small bowl of ashes around. Invite each participant to feel the ashes between their fingers.

Reflection:
Ashes are dirty, gritty, black—the remnant of what remains after something burns and dies. Yet, ashes are the symbol of Christ's victory over death—from the blackness of death comes the bright light of new life.

Question:
To what aspect of your life does this Ash Wednesday challenge you to "die?" How would that "death" change your relationship with God? With friends and family? With yourself?

First Week of Lent

Ritual:
Pass around a bowl of sand or invite the participants to run their hands through a larger bowl or pile of sand.

Reflection:
We often associate sand with the desert. It is dry, lifeless, desperate. Jesus went out into the desert for forty days to pray and fast, only to be tempted by Satan at the very end when he was hungriest, thirstiest, most physically in need.

Question:
What are the three greatest temptations in your life right now—one associated with your relationship with God, one associated with your relationships with others, one associated with your relationship with yourself? In each of the three situations, what do you need from God, from others, and from yourself to prevent you from succumbing to your temptations?

Second Week of Lent

Ritual:
Place the pictures around the room or in the center. Invite the participants to walk around and look at the pictures.

Reflection:
The transfiguration of Jesus on the mountain gives us a hint of and points to Jesus' death on another mountain, Calvary, to a different kind of glory. Peter is dazzled by what he sees and who he recognizes. But God intervenes, reminding the disciples who Jesus is and to listen to him.

Question:
In which people did you easily recognize Jesus? Why? How are you called to respond to those people? In which people did you struggle to see Jesus? Why? How are you called to respond to those people? What do you have to let go of or "die to" in order to see Jesus in those people?

Third Week of Lent

Ritual:
Invite the participants to draw a cup of water from the large bowl and drink it.

Reflection:
Water is the essential element for living. All life needs water to grow and thrive. In the reading from John, Jesus ultimately offers the Samaritan woman living water so that she will never thirst.

Question:
For what in your life are you thirsting?
How can God satisfy your thirst?
What are others in your life thirsting for?
How can you satisfy their thirst?

Fourth Week of Lent

Ritual:
Invite each participant or small groups of participants to light one of the smaller candles, lanterns, or lights and place it in front of them.

Reflection:
One aspect of this reading is the relationship of sin, faith, and both physical and spiritual blindness. Jesus, the light of the world, overcame the darkness of sin by his death.

Question:
How has your faith in God and in Jesus helped you through the times of darkness in your relationships with others?

Fifth Week of Lent

Reflection:
The reading of the raising of Lazarus occurs two weeks before we celebrate the resurrection of our Lord. Jesus brings Lazarus back to his earthly life. As in the Gospels of the Samaritan woman and the man born blind, Jesus offers Lazarus, his sisters, their friends, and his followers something more—new life through him.

Question:
What are the limits that you have around your relationship with God?
Your relationship with friends, family, neighbors, others in the community?
Your relationship with yourself?
What do you need to overcome those limits—from God, from others, from yourself?

Palm Sunday of the Lord's Passion

Ritual:
Give each of the participants a palm frond or shrub branch. Invite them to place them in the center of the prayer space. Process a crucifix or cross into the space and place it in the center of the palms/branches.

Reflection:
Jesus' ride into Jerusalem is the ride to his death. So unlike the parade of a criminal to his execution, this is Jesus' journey to his glory on the cross.

Question:
During the last six weeks, you have walked the Lenten road in prayer, with almsgiving, and in fasting, letting go of those things that prevent you from being in right relationship with God, others, and yourself. As you journey to Easter, what is that last obstacle that you must carry and overcome in order to find new life in your relationships with God, others, and yourself?

CLOSING

Suggested song:

On a Journey Together (Angotti)
  Voices as One Hymnal #69, CD 3 Track 15

EASTER *Easter*

MATERIALS NEEDED

Cut-out fish shapes with the word "ICHTHUS" printed on them

Markers or pens (one per person)

Netting or a large basket

Paschal candle

NOTES

- Set the paschal candle in the center or at the front of the prayer space and place the netting or basket nearby.
- Place cut-out fish and markers or pens near the netting or basket.
- Because this is a season of rejoicing, a more extended gathering rite with multiple songs that the young people can sing is encouraged.

GATHERING

Suggested songs include:

Come, Christians, Unite (Bolduc)
  Voices as One Hymnal #15, CD 1 Track 13
Come! Let Us Sing Out Our Praise (Tate)
  Voices as One Hymnal #17, CD 1 Track 15
He Is Jesus (Bolduc)
  Voices as One Hymnal #34, CD 2 Track 6
Look to the One (Bolduc)
  Voices as One Hymnal #57, CD 3 Track 5

Leader: In the name of the Father,
and of the Son,
and of the Holy Spirit.

All: Amen.

Reading: John 21:1–19

TALKING POINTS

As you break open the Word, some points to share include:

- This is a post-Resurrection encounter between Jesus and Peter found in John's Gospel.
- At this moment in his life, Peter is full of awe and wonder at the Risen Lord—one clue to us as to how to respond to the Resurrection.
- Jesus eats very human food with his friends.
- We see two circles in the relationship between Jesus and Peter being completed.
- Jesus asks Peter, "Do you love me?" three times—a parallel to the three times that Peter denied him.

- Jesus calls Peter to follow him for the second time, reminiscent of Jesus' call to Peter at the beginning of his ministry.
- Jesus clearly demonstrates that he has fulfilled his teachings and promises.
- The challenge for Peter and for us is to follow Jesus even to death.
- Each time that Peter responds "yes" to Jesus' question, Jesus tells Peter to feed others as he has done.
- We know that Peter does as Jesus asks, spreading the good news of Jesus' ministry, death, and resurrection.
- Like Peter, we are called to share the food of ourselves, to nurture others just as Jesus gave his life, his body, so that we might have new life in God.
- The fish is one of the earliest symbols that was used to identify Christians, those who had accepted Jesus' challenge to "feed my sheep."
- The "ICHTHUS" expressed the core of the early Christian community's beliefs—Jesus Christ, God, Savior, Son.

RITUAL

Pass out cut-out "ichthus" fish and markers or pens to each participant.

Invite the participants to reflect on the following questions.

1. How can you be food for others?
2. Who are you being called to feed?

Ask them to write their name and their answers on the back of the fish and place it in the netting or basket. Let them know that their responses will be shared aloud as part of this ritual.

Ask one or more people to read the responses to the first question from the fish in the netting or basket. Remind the participants that this is a listing of the bounty that this group has to give and share with others.

CLOSING

Invite everyone to take their own fish home and give the fish to the person they named or to share the food that they have to give with someone.

Suggested songs include:

God's Love Is Eternal (Tate)
   Voices as One Hymnal #29, CD 2 Track 2

We Will Walk (Bolduc)
   Voices as One Hymnal #102, CD 4 Track 21

SAINTS Feasts of the Saints & Name Days

MATERIALS NEEDED

Baptismal candles (one for each person blessed during the service)—if possible, invite those to be honored to bring their baptismal candle from home.

Paschal candle

NOTES

- This service celebrates the gifts of both particular saints and those named after them. For the sake of reference throughout the service, those named after the saints will be referred to as "honorees."
- Invite the honorees' friends or peers to research the saint for whom the honorees are named. If there is no specific saint, use Jesus as the focus.
- Information about the saint(s) will be used during the ritual part of the service.
- If more than one saint is honored, modify the prayer texts as needed.
- Set up the prayer space so that the participants can sit in a comfortable circle on the floor or in chairs.
- Position the paschal candle near the center of the prayer space.
- Place a baptismal candle, one for each honoree who will be called forth, near the prayer leader.
- Invite the community to sit in a circle as they enter.

GATHERING

Suggested songs include:

Come! Let Us Sing Out Our Praise (Tate)
  Voices as One Hymnal #17, CD 1 Track 15

God So Loved the World (Tate)
  Voices as One Hymnal #27, CD 1 Track 22

He Is Jesus (Bolduc)
  Voices as One Hymnal #34, CD 2 Track 6

Prayer leader lights the paschal candle.

Leader: Please respond "thanks be to God" to the following statement.

Christ is our Light.

All: Thanks be to God.

Leader: Loving God,
Jesus is the light of the world,
the light who has shown us
the way to God.

Today we remember St. _____ who carried your light throughout his/her life, who showed us how to love and forgive, and how to heal and nourish friends, family, neighbors, and strangers. _____ (name of honoree), because you were named for St. _____ , we ask God to give you St. _____'s strength to carry his/her light, to love and forgive, to heal and nourish as Jesus did. We ask this through Christ our Lord.

All: Amen.

Reading: Matthew 5:14–16

TALKING POINTS

As you break open the Word, some points to share include:

- At our baptism, each of us was given a name and a candle.
- The candle serves to remind us that we are called to walk as children of the light.
- Often, our baptismal candle ends up in a drawer, a closet, or a box of memorabilia.
- In this Gospel, Jesus reminds us to bring that light out for all to see so that others will recognize the goodness of God in us and praise God.
- The saint we remember was known for his/her many gifts. (Invite someone to share the qualities, traits, characteristics, or gifts of the saint, and how that person was a light for others.)
- In the ritual that follows, we will relight the baptismal candle and name the gifts of those we honor here.

RITUAL

Place the young person/people named after that saint at the center of the circle.

Light a baptismal candle from the paschal candle for each person and ask him/her to hold it.

Invite each participant to come forward and place a hand on the individual(s)' shoulder or arm and name one gift that that person has shared with others.

If the size of the group allows it, ask the participant to stay standing with their hand on the person while the others come forward to name another gift.

Leader:
>Loving God,
>we thank you for the example
>of St. _____ ,
>who carried your light through his/her life,
>shining your love and mercy on those he/she met.
>We ask you to bless
>_____ (name of honoree).
>Continue to nurture the light of Christ
> within him/her.
>Give him/her the strength
> to enlighten our path to you
>as we walk together as children of the light.
>We ask this through Christ our Lord.

All: Amen.

CLOSING

Suggested songs include:

In the Light (Poirier)
   Voices as One Hymnal #48, CD 2 Track 18

Show Us the Way (Light/Tate)
   Voices as One Hymnal #83, CD 4 Track 5

Blessings for Departure and Return of Those on Pilgrimage

MATERIALS NEEDED

Candle

Ribbons or slips of colored paper (two for each pilgrim)

Pins

Book of Intercessions (optional)

NOTES

- Set prayer space in a circle with the lighted candle at the center.
- Place a table near the door where people enter.
- As people arrive, invite the pilgrims to write their names on two ribbons or slips of paper.
- Separate the ribbons or slips of paper into two piles. Set both piles on the table with the candle.

WHEN THE PILGRIMS DEPART...

GATHERING

Suggested songs include:

He Is Jesus (Bolduc)
   Voices as One Hymnal #34, CD 2 Track 6

Show Us the Way (Light/Tate)
   Voices as One Hymnal #83, CD 4 Track 5

Leader:	In the name of the Father, and of the Son, and of the Holy Spirit.
All:	Amen.
Reading:	Luke 9:1–6

TALKING POINTS

As you break open the Word, some points to share include:

- At this point in his ministry, Jesus commissions the Twelve to do as he did—to preach and heal, to expel demons and cure diseases—by giving them the authority and power to do so.
- He also instructs them to take nothing, and he tells them how to respond to those they meet.
- Luke tells us that they were successful in their preaching and healing.
- This Scripture speaks to us of commissioning and authority.
- In this service, the gathered community commissions the pilgrims to be its emissaries or ambassadors to the larger Catholic or Christian community to which they are going.
- The gathered community will give the pilgrims its "authority" to represent the community and act on its behalf during the pilgrims' journey and at their destination.
- Like Jesus, the gathered community expects the pilgrims to honor the trust they have been given and use it wisely.

- The Gospel reminds us that when we are true to the authority that we have been given, we are able to fulfill our responsibilities to the one who gave it to us.

RITUAL

Leader calls each pilgrim forth by reading from their ribbon or slip of paper and invites them to stand near the candle.

As each name is called, someone pins the ribbon or slip of paper to the candle.

> (Optional: Inscribe the names of the pilgrims in the parish or school Book of Intercessions. This may be done instead of or in addition to pinning the names on the candle with ribbon or slips of paper. Be sure to include an intercession during the Sunday liturgy to pray for the pilgrims while they are gone.)

Leader:

Christ our Light commissioned
his twelve friends to go forth,
giving them full authority to preach and heal,
to spread the good news everywhere they went.

In the same way, Christ calls you to be light
for others as you embark on your journey.

We, the community of _____ ,
declare that you are our ambassadors,
our representatives to the community
that gathers at/in _____ .

We send you forth on this journey.
May Christ's light shine radiantly through you
so that all who meet you may see
   the face of God.
As a sign of our love for you,
we will keep this candle burning
as we pray for you and those with whom
   you walk.

We will not let this light die
   until we see each other again.

Invite the other participants to come forward and place their hands on the shoulders, arms, or heads of the pilgrims.

Leader:

God of the journey,
you summoned your closest friends
and sent them forth
to preach and heal those whom they met.

We ask you to bless these pilgrims
as they travel to _____ .

May your light burn constantly within them
as they share your words of love and forgiveness
with those they meet.

May the Holy Spirit go with them as leave this
place and bring them back to us safely.

We ask this through Christ our Lord.

All: Amen.

CLOSING

Leader:

We the community of _____
send you forth on your pilgrimage to
_____ .

We await your return in _____ days,
when we look forward to being nourished
by the stories of your journey.

Remind everyone where the candle will be placed while the pilgrims are gone. One way to involve the larger parish community would be to place it in a location where the rest of the parish can easily see it.

Invite participants to take the second ribbon or slip of paper home and continue to pray while the pilgrims are gone.

Suggested songs include:

On a Journey Together (Angotti)
   Voices as One Hymnal #69, CD 3 Track 15

Strength for the Journey (Poirier)
   Voices as One Hymnal #87, CD 4 Track 8

We Are the Hope (Tate)
   Voices as One Hymnal #97, CD 4 Track 17

WHEN THE PILGRIMS RETURN...

MATERIALS NEEDED

Candle with the ribbons or slips of paper
One taper for each person
Symbols or objects from the pilgrims' journey

NOTES

- Ensure that the large candle is lit before anyone arrives.
- Set the candle in the center of the prayer space or at the front on a table that can be decorated with symbols from the pilgrims' journey.
- Place tapers alongside the lit candle.

GATHERING

During the gathering song, invite the pilgrims to place symbols or items from their journey on the table with the candle.

Suggested songs include:

On a Journey Together (Angotti)
   Voices as One Hymnal #69, CD 3 Track 15

We Are the Hope (Tate)
   Voices as One Hymnal #97, CD 4 Track 17

Leader: In the name of the Father,
         and of the Son,
         and of the Holy Spirit.

All: Amen.

Leader:
   Gracious God,
   we offer our thanks
   for the safe return of these pilgrims.
   You guided them through their wanderings,
   and brought them back to us,
   filled with your Spirit.
   May we welcome them as openly and lovingly
   as you welcome us to yourself.
   We ask this through Christ our Lord.

All: Amen.

Reading: Luke 9:10–17

TALKING POINTS

As you break open the Word, some points to share include:

- The apostles returned to tell Jesus the stories of their journey. Others listened and crowded around them.
- Eventually, the story leads into the multiplication of the loaves and fishes.
- This connection is a reminder that the food of our journeys must be shared with others so that the good news may be multiplied.

RITUAL

Invite each pilgrim to come forward, one by one, light a taper, then share a story of their experience while being away.

After the last story has been shared, distribute tapers to everyone else.

Invite the pilgrims to light the tapers of the rest of the group.

CLOSING

Leader:
   Christ our Light,
   you called those in our company,
   (name each pilgrim at this point),
   to journey away to _____
   to spread the good news,
   to love and forgive others as you did.

   You return them to us,
   filled with stories of the light they have shared
   and the light that was shared with them.
   Nurture the flame within us all
   that we may continue to share these stories
   and feed those who long for your love
   and compassion.

   We praise you, our Savior Jesus Christ;
   you are Lord for ever and ever.

All: Amen.

Suggested songs include:

He Is Jesus (Bolduc)
   Voices as One Hymnal #34, CD 2 Track 6

Show Us the Way (Light/Tate)
   Voices as One Hymnal #83, CD 4 Track 5

ATHLETICS
Start of Athletic Season

MATERIALS NEEDED

Athlete prayer cards (see notes below)

NOTES

- This prayer service focuses on two pieces of Scripture and small group reflection rather than on a ritual activity.
- It is intended to be a contrast to and a balance for the focus of athletic endeavors on competition.
- Create a business card-size prayer card with the Micah 6:8 and 2 Timothy 4:7 texts on either side of the card for each participant.

GATHERING

Suggested songs include:

Come! Let Us Sing Out Our Praise (Tate)
  Voices as One Hymnal #17, CD 1 Track 15
Glorify the Lord with Me (Tate)
  Voices as One Hymnal #24, CD 1 Track 20

Invite the young people to introduce themselves and if they are an athlete, state what sport they play.

Leader: In the name of the Father,
  and of the Son,
  and of the Holy Spirit.

All: Amen.

Leader:
  Lord of all contests,
  throughout history,
  you gathered your people in many places
  to play games,
  to celebrate victories,
  and to mourn defeats.
  Whether we win or lose,
  you ask only that we keep faith in you
  and love each other.
  We gather today to mark the beginning
    of a new athletic season,
  knowing that there will be many victories
    and many defeats.
  May this season continue to teach us
    to be more like you,
  ever just, ever merciful, ever humble.
  We ask this through Christ our Lord.

All: Amen.

Reading 1: Micah 6:8

Reading 2: 2 Timothy 4:6–8

25

TALKING POINTS

As you break open the Word, some points to share include:

- The reading from Micah is often used when we talk about justice.
- Justice means "that which meets a standard."
- Our standard is God's and Jesus' law—the greatest commandment, to love one another as God has loved us.
- That standard is demonstrated in our behavior toward others, ourselves, and God.
- Competition focuses on standards—scores, times to beat, levels of excellence.
- The Christian call is to a standard of just competition in which doing justice means loving one's neighbor.
- The second part of Micah states that we are to love mercy—to treat others with compassion, ask for forgiveness, and forgive others.
- The third part of Micah states that we are to walk humbly with God in the fullness of our gifts, but with humility and gratitude for what we have been given.
- At the end of a competition, we should strive to be able to repeat and own Paul's words —"I have fought the good fight, I have finished the race, all for the glory of God."

REFLECTION

Divide the young people into three small groups.

Assign each small group one of the three "requirements" of Micah 6:8—doing justice, being merciful, and being humble—as the focus for the questions below.

1. In what ways can we demonstrate our "requirement" in our daily lives in school, at home, with friends, among strangers, at work?
2. In what ways can we demonstrate our "requirement" during our athletic activities?
3. What experiences in our athletic activities make it a challenge to live up to this "requirement?" Think about specific past experiences when you found it difficult to fulfill your group's "requirement."

Invite the small groups to share their responses to the first three questions with the large group.

4. Ask the young people to reflect on the final question individually, then share their answers with the large group.
5. Which is the greatest challenge for me in my athletic experience—doing justice, being merciful, or being humble? Why?

Intercessions

Leader: **As we begin this athletic season, we hold our prayers up to our God, confident that God will hear them.**

Response: Lord, hear our prayer.

> For all of those who compete,
>   we pray to the Lord . . .
> For the family and friends who celebrate with and console our athletes,
>   we pray to the Lord . . .
> For the coaches and officials who guide our athletes on the field,
>   we pray to the Lord . . .
> For the managers, trainers, and groundskeepers who support our athletes,
>   we pray to the Lord . . .
> For the strength to do justice, love mercy, and walk humbly before God on and off the field of play,
>   we pray to the Lord . . .
> For the courage to run the race and fight the good fight with steadfast faith in God,
>   we pray to the Lord . . .

CLOSING

Distribute the prayer cards to everyone. Encourage them to keep the card in their wallet and pray either verse before a game or match.

Suggested songs include:

Christ Be Near at Either Hand (arr. Gillen)
   Voices as One Hymnal #14, CD 1 Track 12

I Will Praise Your Name (Bolduc)
   Voices as One Hymnal #44, CD 2 Track 14

Show Us the Way (Light/Tate)
   Voices as One Hymnal #83, CD 4 Track 5

ATHLETICS
Prayer at the Start of an Athletic Game

MATERIALS NEEDED

None

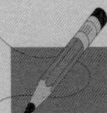
NOTES

- This prayer service is intended to be repeated at the start of any athletic game or event.
- To facilitate easy repetition, the readings and prayers are deliberately short.
- To facilitate easy memorization, the text of the service can be printed on a prayer card or business card and distributed to the young people.
- In the third line of the litany, fill in the name of the patron saint of the school or parish.

GATHERING

Leader: In the name of the Father, and of the Son, and of the Holy Spirit.

All: Amen.

Reading 1: Psalm 27:1

Reading 2: Philippians 4:8

Litany

Jesus, mighty God.

Response: Have mercy on us.

Mary, mirror of justice.

Response: Pray for us.

_____, patron and guide.

Response: Pray for us.

Our Father...

Beginning of the School Year

MATERIALS NEEDED

School books (various subjects)

Blank prayer cards or business-card size cards (enough for three cards per person)

Pens or markers

Bookmarks of saints (optional; see "Closing" for more information)

NOTES

- Invite the young people to bring their school books to the service. (Remind them to put their names in their books.)
- As they enter, ask them to stack their books by subject in various areas around the room.
- The cards will be used to connect those who are strong in certain subjects with those who are weak in the same subjects. To maintain that connection, it would be valuable for the young people to stay in touch with each other to support each other. We suggest using phone numbers or e-mail addresses. If safety is a concern, the leader may suggest other alternatives for keeping in touch—locker numbers or a common "mail drop" at the campus ministry or youth ministry office or in a classroom. The campus/youth minister or teacher might be responsible for distributing notes to the young people.
- The young people are asked to fill out two cards on their strong subject so that everyone's "weak subject" will match up with someone else's "strong subject."

GATHERING

Suggested songs include:

I Will Praise Your Name (Bolduc)
    Voices as One Hymnal #44, CD 2 Track 14

Lift Your Hearts to the Holy One (Light/Tate)
    Voices as One Hymnal #56, CD 3 Track 4

Leader: In the name of the Father,
            and of the Son,
            and of the Holy Spirit.

All: Amen.

Reading 1: 2 Corinthians 12:7b–10

TALKING POINTS

As you break open the Word, some points to share include:

- Paul writes about a paradox—being strong in his weakness.
- He asks God to deliver him from his weakness, but is told that God's grace is enough because God's power comes to its fullness in weakness.
- Paul realizes that when he admits and lives with his weaknesses, then he is more open to God's presence and activity in his life—and that is true strength.
- God has given each of us different gifts in school.
- We are called to be the living presence of God—grace—for each other, to actively help those whose weakness is our strength.

REFLECTION ACTIVITY

Part One

Invite the young people to sit by the books that represent their strongest or best subject.

Pass out the three cards and a pen or markers to each person.

- Ask them to write their name and phone number/e-mail address on each card
- Ask them to write the word "strength" on the blank side of one card. Beneath the word "strength," ask them to write the name of the subject where they are sitting.
- Ask them to reflect on the following question, then write their answer on the side of the card that says, "strength."

1. Why is this subject my best or strongest subject?

With one or two people (some groups may be large), invite them to share their response to the question, then ask the pairs to share their partner's response with the others sitting in their group.

Invite the young people to sit by another subject in which they are strong and write that on the second card.

- Ask them to reflect on question 1 a second time and share their response with a partner.
- Have them keep both cards.
- Ask everyone to find the books that represent their weakest or hardest subject.
- Ask them to write the word "weakness" on the blank side of the last card. Underneath the word "weakness," ask them to write the name of the subject where they are sitting.
- Ask them to reflect on the following questions, write their answer to number 3 on the card, then share their responses with their group.

2. Why is this subject my weakest or hardest subject?
3. What kind of help do I need or in what areas do I need help to do better in this subject area?

The goal of the next step is for each "weak subject" person to pair up with their corresponding "strong subject" person. This can be accomplished in a variety of ways.

- Invite the young people to find someone whose strong subject is their weak subject.
- In the large group, invite each young person individually to name their weak subject and find their corresponding partner.
- Lay out the cards on a table or on the floor and invite everyone to find the card of someone whose strong subject is their weak one.

Once they have found the person whose strong subject is their weak subject, ask them to sit next to that person. As people find each other, a circle should naturally form.

Reading 2:   1 Corinthians 13:2

TALKING POINTS

As you break open the Word, some points to share include:

- During this process, we identified some of the academic gifts that we have to share with others.
- In this reading, Paul reminds us that these gifts, especially knowledge, are from God.
- Though we may know everything and have the most faith, if we don't know how to share our gifts with others, then they are empty gifts.
- We are called to share our gifts of knowledge with others in love.
- The challenge we face at the start of the school year is being God's loving presence—grace and strength—in the weakness of others.

REFLECTION ACTIVITY

Part Two

Starting with one person in the circle, ask each participant to do the following.

- Turn to the person next to him/her whose weak subject is their strong subject.
- Exchange "strong subject" and "weak subject" cards.
- Invite the "strong subject" person to read the response to question 3 (what kind of help I need to do better) quickly and silently.

- Then invite the "strong subject" person to say what they would be willing to do to support that person in that subject area. Possibilities include tutoring if needed, corresponding by e-mail, praying for the person.

Intercessions

During the second part of the intercessions, the participants will be invited to ask God for gifts that they need to help or support them as they try to be God's loving, gracious presence with others during the school year. The leader will start with two intercessions as a model for possible responses.

Leader: Let us join our voices in prayer.
Our response is "Pray for us."

St. Joseph of Cupertino, a mystic, who lacked book knowledge but was gifted with insight. R/.

St. Francis de Sales, priest and scholar, who served the weakest and poorest in the cities with kindness and generosity. R/.

St. Bonaventure, bishop and teacher, who combined a life of tender piety and profound learning. R/.

St. Alphonsus Liguori, lawyer, bishop, theologian, missionary, and mystic, who preached the Word of God to goatherds and instructed the unlearned. R/.

St. Thomas Aquinas, patron of all Catholic universities, academies, colleges, and schools, who embraced academic work as the way to great understanding of God. R/.

St. Teresa of Avila, mystic, who used her physical weaknesses as an opportunity to understand God through prayer and visions. R/.

St. Dominic, preacher, who sold his books to feed the poor and sold himself into slavery to liberate others. R/.

St. Catherine of Siena, writer and politician, who without formal education guided the work and lives of princes and popes. R/.

St. Anthony of Padua, who, though highly educated, did not boast of his knowledge, but only his desire to serve the Lord. R/.

Blessed Kateri Tekakwitha, who learned and practiced her faith despite the sin and deprivation that surrounded her. R/.

St. Elizabeth Ann Seton, mother and foundress, who read and wrote letters, journals, and translations so that others might understand the fire in her soul for God. R/.

Leader: Our response is,
"Lord, hear our prayer."

For courage, we pray…

For humility, we pray…

Invite the participants to add their prayers spontaneously.

CLOSING

Our Father…

Invite the young people to take the card they received.

Give out bookmarks of the above-named saints (purchased or handmade.) Handmade ones might include the prayer above.

SCHOOL
Prayer Before Homecoming or Prom

MATERIALS NEEDED

Bible

Food and beverages for concluding party

For prom service, create durable prayer cards with the text from Hebrews on it (if possible).

NOTES

- This prayer service works best if both parts are done during the year.
- School banners and symbols as well as balloons, streamers, and other party decorations can be used for the environment.

GATHERING

(for both services)

Suggested background music includes popular songs like "Celebrate" or songs with words that focus on coming home (for homecoming) or endings/going forth (for prom).

Liturgical music to sing includes:

Come, Christians, Unite (Bolduc)
  Voices as One Hymnal #15, CD 1 Track 13

Come! Let Us Sing Out Our Praise (Tate)
  Voices as One Hymnal #17, CD 1 Track 15

Great One in Three (Tate/Berrell)
  Voices as One Hymnal #30, CD 2 Track 3

He Is Jesus (Bolduc)
  Voices as One Hymnal #34, CD 2 Track 6

I Have Been Anointed (Warner)
  Voices as One Hymnal #42, CD 2 Track 12

I Will Praise Your Name (Bolduc)
  Voices as One Hymnal #44, CD 2 Track 14

Before Homecoming

Reading: Acts 4:32–35

REFLECTION

As you break open the Word, some points to share include:

- For the early Christians, coming together was a time of great rejoicing.
- They brought everything they had to the gathering of the community to share with each other.
- They also shared their faith openly and, because of it, they were respected.

REFLECTION QUESTION 1

Break into small groups of three or four people. Ask the groups to share their responses to the following question.

31

Describe one or two experiences that you had over the summer that were important to you.

Continue the reflection with these points:

- Coming together for the early Christians also meant giving their material goods to each other to hold in common.
- When someone was in need, they helped each other without thinking twice about it.
- The actions of the early Christians challenge our sense of individualism and materialism, especially as we prepare for homecoming.

REFLECTION QUESTION 2

In the same small groups, ask the youth to share their responses to the following questions.

1. As you celebrate the start of the new year, what gifts are you going to share with your friends at school, your family, your co-workers, and/or your parish youth group?
2. How are you going to be the presence of Christ in your various communities?

Prayer

Invite the participants to bow their heads or place their hands on the shoulders of someone near them.

Leader:
> Lord of all joyful gatherings,
> the early Christians were filled with joy
>   whenever they gathered,
> sharing whatever they had with each other,
> being the presence of Jesus Christ
>   in their community.
> We ask you to bless us as we come together
>   at the start of this school year.
> Inspire us to dance and give thanks
>   for all that you have given us.
> Show us how to be generous
>   with everything that we have.
> Help us respond quickly and openly
>   to those in need
> so that we might bring the presence
>   of the Risen Lord to others.
> We ask this through Christ our Lord.

All: Amen.

Before Prom

Reading: Hebrews 13:1–6

REFLECTION

As you break open the Word, some points to share include:

- These words are among the last in the Letter to the Hebrews.
- They are imperatives—commands—to the community, and a summary of the most important points to remember.
- The key commands are: Love one another, welcome strangers, help the needy, be faithful in your relationships, do not be greedy, and remember that God is all you need.

REFLECTION QUESTIONS

Break into small groups of three or four people. Ask the groups to share their responses to the following questions.

1. During the past year, which command has been easiest for you to obey? What are some examples of how have you lived out that command this year?
2. Which command has been the most difficult for you this year? Why has it been hard to obey it?
3. For which command do you need the prayers and support of this community during the summer and next year?

Prayer

In preparation for this prayer, invite the participants to identify someone in their lives, an adult or young person, who has been an example of God's commands to us throughout this past school year. They will be asked to call out those names in the middle of the prayer. Also, the participants will be asked to share the command for which they need prayer and support during the summer and next year.

Leader:
> Faithful God,
> you sent us your Son, Jesus,
>   to show us how to live your love.
> He taught us how to love one another,
>   how to welcome the stranger
>   and help the needy,
> how to be faithful in our relationships
>   and not be greedy.

He showed us your faithfulness
   by being faithful to us,
and gave all that he had,
including his life,
to remind us that we have all that we need.
At the end of this year,
during this time of celebration,
we thank you for the people in our lives
who have shown us the face of God
   throughout this year.

We thank you for:
(Participants spontaneously call out names.)

As this school year comes to a close and we look ahead, we turn to you to ask for your strength to continue to live out your commands.

We need to continue to learn how to:
(Participants spontaneously call out their response to the third reflection question.)

We ask these things through your Son,
   Jesus Christ,
who is Lord forever and ever.

All: Amen.

CLOSING

End these prayer services with a party that includes food, beverages, and dancing.

SCHOOL: Prayer Before Exams

MATERIALS NEEDED

Small wooden crosses (one for each participant)—these could be constructed of simple materials like tongue depressors or clean twigs

Fabric paint (preferred) or markers

NOTES

- The reading for this service is Jesus' agony in the garden. Without preparation, it may sound odd or misplaced. The gathering is an opportunity to establish the connection between the young people's experiences at this time and Jesus' critical moment.
- The space should be open and large enough so that the young people can lie on the floor or sit comfortably in chairs with some room between them.
- Place a cross or crucifix in a prominent place in the prayer space. The smaller crosses could be placed in a basket or scattered around the base of the larger cross.

GATHERING

Suggested songs include:

All Will Be Well (Warner)
   Voices as One Hymnal #1, CD 1 Track 1
Hear Me, O God (Tate)
   Voices as One Hymnal #35, CD 2 Track 7
We Gather Here (Bolduc)
   Voices as One Hymnal #99, CD 4 Track 18

Leader: In the name of the Father,
            and of the Son,
            and of the Holy Spirit.

All: Amen.

Invite the young people to share their immediate responses to the following questions:

1. What are the kinds of things that you ask God for right now as you study and prepare for exams?
2. What are the emotions that you are feeling as you look ahead toward exams?

Leader: Let us pray.
>
> Loving God,
> we gather together today,
> weighed down by the stress and anxiety
>   of exam time.
> We come here,
> confident that you hear our needs,
> and trusting that you will help us bear these loads.
> Open our minds to the challenges of these days
> and open our hearts to humbly accept
>   your grace.
> We ask this through Christ our Lord.

All: Amen.

Reading: Matthew 26:36–39

TALKING POINTS

As you break open the Word, some points to share include:

- The agony in the garden is Jesus' "end-of-semester test," in a sense. It is the moment when all that he has said, done, and stood for either comes together or falls apart, depending upon how he chooses to face it.
- Jesus takes his friends with him, and asks them to do three things: stay awake, keep watch, and pray.
- Like Jesus, you have prepared the entire semester/year for these exams, and like him, you can't avoid them.
- Many of you probably have chosen to study with friends, hoping that they will stay awake into the late hours, keep you focused, and even pray when the subject seems too difficult.
- Jesus saw what was ahead of him—death—but he also knew that the new life of the Resurrection followed. He saw his "test" as one important step in a bigger journey.
- While exams might feel like a "crucifixion" of sorts, we know that there is "new life" after them—a passing grade, a finished class, a feeling of satisfaction, an "aha!" experience because you learned something.
- As you face exams ahead and the work involved, you have a choice—to pull all that you have learned together and study, or let it all fall apart.
- What is clear for both Jesus and you is that where we are today is the result of all of the work that we have (or have not) done during the past months.
- Jesus built a life so that in death he could carry our sins and weaknesses.
- In these moments and next few days, we pray that we can give our stresses and weaknesses to Jesus to carry while we continue to do the work of building our academic lives.

REFLECTION—GUIDED IMAGERY

Invite the young people to get into a comfortable and relaxed position. It would be ideal if they could spread out on the floor.

Ask them to uncross hands, legs, and feet, and close their eyes. Encourage them to focus on the rhythm of their breathing.

Begin the following text.

> Imagine that you are on a building work site—perhaps rehabbing a house for Habitat for Humanity or at your parish/school's work camp location. Off in the distance is a pile of lumber of many different sizes and lengths, everything from long 4 x 4-inch posts to scraps of 1 x 1-inch. You've been assigned a project in which you will be building a platform for all of the knowledge and tools that you will need to succeed at any school subject of your choosing. This platform will be built of wood and must be able to hold the weight of all the knowledge, the tools, the struggles, the challenges that you face in learning this subject. The manager of the project asks you to select pieces of wood from the pile that you will need to build this platform, then move those pieces closer to the site. As you look at the pile, which pieces do you need? Pick up the pieces that you need and start to move them closer to your work site. Which pieces are easy to move? Which pieces are difficult?

At this point, invite the participants to open their eyes.

Invite them to reflect on the following questions. Their responses can be shared with a partner or in a small group.

1. For what subject was your platform?
2. What kind of lumber did your platform need in order to hold everything?
3. Which pieces of lumber were easy to move? Which ones were difficult? Why?

Remind the young people that we are called to build the foundations and carry the lumber of our own lives, but Jesus is here to help us face the challenges. It is through the ultimate symbol of the cross that we remember that Jesus bears our heaviest burdens.

ACTIVITY

Invite the young people to take one of the small wooden crosses and fabric paint or a marker.

- Ask them to write two things on the cross: the name of their most challenging subject and their biggest fear or concern about exams.
- In the background, play soft instrumental music.

Intercessory Prayer

This prayer has two parts.
The response for both parts is, "Hear us, O Lord."

Part 1

Invite the young people to name their most challenging subject.

Part 2

Invite the young people to name their fear or concern about exams.

Leader:
>Hear us, O Lord,
>as we lay our burdens and struggles before you.
>Give us courage and strength,
>especially during these exam times,
>to build the lives that you call us to
>with the lumber you have given us.
>Help us bear the challenges and fears
>   of these exams
>as you bravely bore your own cross.
>We ask this through Christ our Lord.

All: Amen.

CLOSING

Our Father...

Invite the young people to place their crosses at the foot of the large cross.

Suggested song:

Strength for the Journey (Poirier)
  Voices as One Hymnal #87, CD 4 Track 8

SCHOOL: Blessing of Graduates

MATERIALS NEEDED

Large sticks (branches from trees or cut pieces of 1 x 1-inch, approximately 39-inches tall)—one per graduate

Stapler and staples or cellophane tape

Various colored slips of paper (8.5 x 11-inch paper cut into eighths)

Full sheets of 8.5 x 11-inch paper

Pens or markers

Symbols or objects that represent what awaits the graduates in the next 5–10 years—college paraphernalia, marriage/children, armed services, trade schools, new home

NOTES

- Clear a space for this prayer service that is free of chairs or other furniture.

- At the front of the space, extend a line of fabric, colored paper, or some other objects that might remind the participants of a river the width of the prayer space a few feet from the front of the prayer space. On the narrow bank of the "river," set up symbols or objects that represent what awaits the graduates in the next 5–10 years—college paraphernalia, marriage/children, armed services, trade schools, new home.

- Everyone will sit on the wide bank of the "river," facing the arranged objects.

- Place the walking sticks around the floor. Be sure to put the name of a graduate clearly on each stick. The name could be painted on with fabric paint, carved into the wood roughly, or written on a piece of paper that is stapled to the stick.

- The gathering rite will take some time, especially if there are a number of graduates. Have sufficient background music to set the atmosphere.

- Depending upon the size of the group, each young person might fill out a slip of paper for only a couple of graduates rather than all of the graduates.

GATHERING

Suggested songs include:
Live in Me (Bolduc)
   Voices as One Hymnal #55, CD 3 Track 3
Strength for the Journey (Poirier)
   Voices as One Hymnal #87, CD 4 Track 8

Young People (not graduates)

As the young people come into the space, invite them to take slips of paper (one for each graduate) and a pen or marker, and write down their response to one of the following statements for each graduate.

> I want to thank you and affirm you for . . .
> One of the things that I will always remember about you is . . .

Ask the young people to staple or tape their slips of paper to the appropriate stick for each graduate.

Bring the completed walking sticks towards the "river's edge" for use later in the service.

Graduates

As the graduates arrive, invite them to take paper and a pen or marker, and respond to the following reflection questions.

1. What were some of the events or experiences with this community that had a significant impact on you during the past four years? How did they affect or change you?

2. What were some of the significant challenges you faced during the last four years? How did they challenge you to grow?

3. What were the significant moments of celebration this community shared with you?

Leader:
> We gather together
> as our graduates are looking ahead
> and back at the same time.
> We gather to celebrate the completion
>   of their journey to graduation
> and to say good-bye and thank you
>   for leading the way,
> especially during the past year.

Let us pray.
> God of the journey,
> you called your people Israel
> out of a strange country to a new land
>   of promise and hope.
> Along the way,
> they were led by Moses,
> but as they looked across
>   at their future and destiny
> you gave them a new leader, Joshua.
> Today we gather as one community
> at the end of this part of the journey
> with these graduates.
> We have walked with them,
> leading them to this point.
> We stand at the edge of the new land ahead
> ready to send them on, led by others.
> May we rejoice and celebrate our arrival together
> at the beginning of the next steps in the road.
> We ask this through Christ our Lord.

All: Amen.

Reading: Deuteronomy 34:1–8

TALKING POINTS

As you break open the Word, some points to share include:

- The last chapter of Deuteronomy, with its account of the death of Moses and the anointing of Joshua as the Israelites' new leader, captures the tension between endings and new beginnings.
- Graduation time has a similar dynamic.
- Both the Israelites and the graduates have been on a long, extended journey toward a "promised land" of wealth and opportunity.
- The journeys have been filled with celebrations as well as difficulties along the way.
- At this point, the community brings its work of nurturing the graduates to an end.

REFLECTION

Invite the graduates to share their responses to the questions from the gathering rite.

RITUAL

- Make the transition from the graduates' reflections by reminding them that they have shared with us some of the stories of our journey together as a community.
- Invite each of the graduates to come forward one at a time.
- Ask some of the other members of the community to read the affirmations, thanks, and memories that they wrote about the graduate.
- Share with the graduates that this walking stick is the community's gift to them as they continue their journey, and that the slips of paper on the stick are reminders of who they have become on this part of their journey.
- When each of the graduates has received their walking stick, invite them to come forward as a group and stand at the center of the community.
- Invite the other members of the community to come forward and place their hands on the head or shoulders of the graduates in a sign of blessing.

Reading: Deuteronomy 34:9

Leader:
> Gracious and loving God,
> bless these graduates,
> our leaders and companions on this journey.
> Give them wisdom and insight
> to choose the right paths.
> Give them strength to follow your way
> as they continue to grow in your love
>   and knowledge.
> We ask this through your Son, Jesus Christ,
>   who is Lord forever and ever.

All: Amen.

CLOSING

Suggested songs include:

On a Journey Together (Angotti)
  Voices as One Hymnal #69, CD 3 Track 15

Strength for the Journey (Poirier)
  Voices as One Hymnal #87, CD 4 Track 8

SCHOOL Baccalaureate

MATERIALS NEEDED

Pieces of elastic, 15-inches long (one per person) or thin cording for a necklace, 24-inches long (one per person)

Beads: four different colors, one of each color per person

Baskets for the beads and elastic/cording (5 or 6 total)

Tape(s) or CD(s) of the senior class song(s)

Book of the Gospels

NOTES

- Ask four graduating seniors to prepare a short witness (1–3 minutes) about how their experience has been similar to each of the four types of soil from the parable.
- If possible, seniors could wear their caps and gowns or something else that represents their school.
- Identify the colored bead that represents each type of soil and share that with the seniors who will be speaking.
- Place the baskets of beads in the front or at the center of the prayer space.

GATHERING

- Play the class song(s) of the seniors participating in this service as young people enter.
- Line up the seniors in a procession outside the prayer space. Give the senior at the front the Book of the Gospels to process into the service.

During the procession, suggested songs include:

Come, Christians, Unite! (Bolduc)
   Voices as One Hymnal #15, CD 1 Track 13

Lift Your Hearts to the Holy One (Light/Tate)
   Voices as One Hymnal #56, CD 3 Track 4

Leader: In the name of the Father,
          and of the Son,
          and of the Holy Spirit.

All: Amen.

Leader:

   God of all Creation,
      you gave us these hearts and bodies
      as fertile soil,
      nurtured by your grace
      to do your work of love and mercy.
   Today we celebrate the rich harvest
      we have in our graduates.
   May we praise and thank you
      for their model and service
   and may we continue to be sowers of your Word.
   We ask this through Christ our Lord.

All: Amen.

Reading: Mark 4:1–20

TALKING POINTS

As you break open the Word, some points to share include:

- As with other parables of the Kingdom, the main character, the sower, is God, who sends the Word, his Son Jesus, to us.
- How we receive the Word into our lives varies.
- The four types of soil represent the four ways in which we hear and nurture the Word of God in our lives:
  (1) The pathway is where the Word is disregarded, crushed, not given a chance to be heard.
  (2) The rocky ground is where the Word is initially heard, where we say, "That's nice," then forget what we have heard the first time someone questions us.
  (3) The thorns are where the Word actually starts to take root, but the other concerns of life—sports teams, homework, colleges, relationships—take over and kill the growing seed.
  (4) The good soil is where we hear the Word, take it to heart, and try to live it every day.
- During the last four years of high school, each of us has had experiences of being each type of soil.

WITNESSES

Invite the first senior to speak to come forward.

As each speaker comes forward, they should take the bead that represents the type of soil, hold it, tell the group what it represents, then share their story.

Ask each senior to name the gift that they needed then and continue to need now in order to become good soil. For the "good soil" witness, ask that speaker to name what gift is needed to continue to be open to the Word of God. The gifts that they name will be used in the ritual that follows.

RITUAL

- Pass out a length of elastic or cording to each young person, including the seniors.
- Invite the seniors to come forward and take a basket of beads. If there are more than four seniors, the baskets can be subdivided into smaller portions. If there are fewer than four seniors, invite the participants to come forward rather than having the one senior pass out all of the beads. If this is a group composed solely of seniors, select four members of the class.
- If the group is sitting in a circle, ask them to stand. If the group is sitting in a theater or auditorium-style setting, situate the four seniors in various places in the front, around the sides, even in the back, and invite the participants to walk from one person to the other to receive their beads.
- As the seniors distribute the beads, they will say, "May God give you the gift of _____."
- As the young people return to their places, invite them to string the beads on their elastic or cording, knot the ends and place it around their wrist or neck.

CLOSING

Leader:

> Creator God,
> you have given us these graduates,
> who have shared with us their joys and struggles
> in sowing the Word in their daily lives.
> May these beads remind us
> that we, too, are soil that must nurture
>   the precious seeds of your Word.
> May we always turn to you
> to seek the nourishment
> of your gracious love and mercy
> and let your seeds take root and flourish
>   in our lives.
> We ask this through your Son, Jesus Christ,
>   who is Lord for ever and ever.

All: Amen.

Suggested songs include:

God's Love Is Eternal (Tate)
   Voices as One Hymnal #29, CD 2 Track 2

Show Us the Way (Light/Tate)
   Voices as One Hymnal #83, CD 4 Track 5

STRESS
Prayer in Time of Stress

MATERIALS NEEDED

Bible

Symbols of school, family, work, sports—books, uniforms, etc.

Leaders: One reader

NOTES

- Set up the room so that the floor area is cleared.
- Invite the participants to pile their symbols in the center of the room and sit in a circle around the pile.

GATHERING

As people are gathering, music might be played in the background or sung. Suggested selections:

Answer Me (Bolduc)
   Voices as One Hymnal #4, CD 1 Track 4

Harbor of My Heart (Warner)
   Voices as One Hymnal #31, CD 2 Track 4

I Turn to You (Mattingly)
   Voices as One Hymnal #43, CD 2 Track 13

In the Arms of the Shepherd (Weckler)
   Voices as One Hymnal #47, CD 2 Track 17

Introduce the topic of stress as one that everyone deals with. Share why this topic is particularly appropriate right now.

Leader: In the name of the Father, and of the Son, and of the Holy Spirit.

All: Amen.

Reading: Matthew 11:28–30

REFLECTION

As you break open the Word, some points to share include:

- We are on a lifelong journey of faith.
- Throughout that journey, we accumulate experiences that energize us and burden us.
- Sometimes our burdens overwhelm us, and we find ourselves focusing on the burden and forgetting about the journey.
- Jesus offers to bear our burdens.
- When stressed, we are challenged to give our burdens over to Jesus.

REFLECTION QUESTIONS

Break into small groups of three or four people.
Ask the groups to share their responses to the following:

Name one burden that you are carrying right now.

Why is it weighing you down?

INTERCESSION ACTIVITY

Invite the participants to take the objects in the middle of the room and build a pathway from one side to the other.

- The pathway should bend and the edges of the path can be of different heights.
- As the intercessions, ask each participant to walk through the path and say the name of the person whose burden they are going to carry in prayer this week.
- Play a song throughout these intercessions.

Suggested songs include:

Answer Me (Bolduc)
   Voices as One Hymnal #4, CD 1 Track 4

Come Home (Mattingly)
   Voices as One Hymnal #16, CD 1 Track 14

Crux Fidelis (Warner)
   Voices as One Hymnal #19, CD 1 Track 16

Hear Me, O God (Tate)
   Voices as One Hymnal #35, CD 2 Track 7

Holy You (Cooney)
   Voices as One Hymnal #38, CD 2 Track 9

In You, O Lord (Bolduc)
   Voices as One Hymnal #49, CD 2 Track 19

Journey for Home (Bolduc)
   Voices as One Hymnal #50, CD 2 Track 20

CLOSING

Leader:
   (Invite everyone to hold hands.)
   Loving God,
   you sent your Son, Jesus,
     to comfort us when we are burdened,
   to remind us that you alone can carry
     all the stresses in our lives.
   Open our eyes so that we might see
     your Son's outstretched hands
   in our families and friends,
   waiting to bear whatever weighs us down.
   As we hold hands today,
   remind us that Jesus calls us
     to bear each other's burdens.
   Help us be the hands
     that hold and carry each other
   during these stressful times.
   We ask this through your Son, Jesus Christ,
   who is Lord forever and ever.

All: Amen.

Suggested songs include:

Be with Me, Lord (Mattingly)
   Voices as One Hymnal #10, CD 1 Track 8

Glorify the Lord with Me (Tate)
   Voices as One Hymnal #24, CD 1 Track 20

God's Love Is Eternal (Tate)
   Voices as One Hymnal #29, CD 2 Track 2

Let Us Sing (Bolduc)
   Voices as One Hymnal #54, CD 3 Track 2

Lift Your Hearts to the Holy One (Light/Tate)
   Voices as One Hymnal #56, CD 3 Track 4

LEADERSHIP
Commissioning of Leaders

MATERIALS NEEDED

Graffiti board (2–3 foot x 4–foot
or 3–foot x 6–foot pieces of foamboard)

One table for each piece of foamboard

Markers

Polaroid™ camera or digital camera

Symbol of each ministry for each leader
Suggestions include a general symbol like a cross, or pins or pendants with a symbol of each ministry. Pins and pendants are sold by many Christian and Catholic bookstores.

NOTES

- Somewhere on the foamboard, write the word "Leadership" in large letters.
- Set up the tables in the gathering area with plenty of different-colored markers nearby.
- At the front or center of the prayer space, set out symbols of the various types of ministry for which leaders will be commissioned, e.g., Bible, instruments, and tools. Designate a place for the graffiti boards to rest when they are brought to the front or center of the prayer space.
- Prepare the youth community for their response ("Yes") to the leader's question during the blessing ritual.

GATHERING

- As the young people enter, invite them to write characteristics of leadership on a graffiti board.
- Ask the youth leaders to stay outside of the prayer space until the beginning of the service.
- Ask the youth leaders to serve as greeters and ministers of hospitality while the other young people gather.
- Once the young people are gathered, invite the youth leaders to review the list of leadership characteristics and choose one that they hope to share with the community in their leadership role.
- Select as many youth leaders as needed to process the graffiti boards into the prayer space during the gathering song, followed by the rest of the youth leaders.

Suggested songs include:

Come, Christians, Unite! (Bolduc)
　Voices as One Hymnal #15, CD 1 Track 13

I Will Praise Your Name (Bolduc)
　Voices as One Hymnal #44, CD 2 Track 14

Lift Your Hearts to the Holy One (Light/Tate)
　Voices as One Hymnal #56, CD 3 Track 4

Leader: In the name of the Father,
and of the Son,
and of the Holy Spirit.

All: Amen.

Leader:
We gather today to bless
　and commission our leaders
to serve this community
　as disciples of Jesus Christ.

Let us pray.
> God of the call,
> throughout our history
> you called many people
> to break open your word,
> to lead us in prayer and praise,
> to guide us to you,
> to serve others in your world.
>
> These young people have heard your call
> to teach, sing, proclaim, welcome,
>   and serve this community.
>
> May they continue to open their hearts
> to the fullness of your call.
>
> We ask this through your Son, Jesus Christ,
> who is Lord forever and ever.

All: Amen.

Reading: John 13:1–7

TALKING POINTS

As you break open the Word, some points to share include:

- As Jesus washed the feet of his disciples, he demonstrated how he expected them to lead and serve others.
- Jesus closely linked leadership and service. In other Gospel accounts in Matthew and Mark, Jesus tells James and John that leadership is about serving the least among us, and that the only glory in leadership is the glory of the cross.
- Jesus demonstrates many qualities of leadership, such as humility, perseverance, and courage, especially in this Gospel.
- As Jesus demonstrates, leadership comes with a price—risking one's life for the sake of others.
- Each of us responds to God's call to leadership through service in different ways.

REFLECTION

Invite different young people to proclaim the following Scriptures about how people have responded to God's call.

As the young people listen to these verses, ask them to decide whose response to God is most like their own.

> Ruth 1:16–18
> 1 Samuel 3:8–10
> Isaiah 6:5–8
> Jeremiah 1:4–8
> Matthew 4:18–22
> Luke 24: 30–35

Divide the young people up according to which Scripture they selected.

Invite them to reflect on the following questions and share them in their group.

1. How would you characterize the response of the individual in the Scripture story to God's call?
2. How is your response to God's call to leadership in this community the same as that person's in the Scripture? How is it different?
3. What characteristic, trait, or gift do you need from God in order to respond to God's call and be a better leader in this community?

Ask each small group to share their responses with the large group.

Reading: John 13:7–17

RITUAL

Call forth the youth leaders by name. Ask them to stand at the front or center of the prayer space.

Leader:
> **Community of _____,**
>   *(name of school/parish)*
> **these young people come here today**
> **having heard God's call to serve you as leaders.**
>
> **Are you prepared to follow them**
>   **along the way of Christ**
> **and to challenge them to continue**
>   **to respond to God's call?**

All: Yes.

Leader: *(To the youth leaders)*
    Your peers have declared their willingness
    to support you as leaders.

    As you came in,
    they wrote down many characteristics
    of leadership.

    As a sign of your commitment
    to this community,
    I ask each of you to name the characteristic
    that you hope to share
    through your leadership.

Each youth leader should name the leadership characteristic individually.

Blessing and Commissioning

Invite the young people to extend both of their hands in a sign of blessing over the youth leaders.

Leader:
    Almighty God,
    through pillars of cloud and fire,
    through visions and dreams,
    through angels and humans,
    you called your people to love you,
    to serve you, to praise you,
    and to worship you.

    Bless these young people
    who have heard your voice in their hearts
    and chosen to love and serve you
    in this grateful community.

    May they lead us to your Kingdom
    as humble servants like Jesus,
    proclaiming your word
    with their mouths
    and through their lives.

    We ask this through your Son, Jesus Christ,
    who is Lord forever and ever.

All: Amen.

Leader:
    This community commissions you as leaders
    and sends you forth to live out the ministry
    to which you have been called.

Call each youth leader forward and name their specific ministry to the community where applicable (e.g., liturgical ministry, service, catechist).

Give each youth leader a symbol of their ministry.

CLOSING

Suggested song:

Show Us the Way (Light/Tate)
    Voices as One Hymnal #83, CD 4 Track 5

- Take Polaroid™ or digital pictures of each of the leaders who were commissioned.
- Glue the photos near the leadership characteristic that the individual named, or post the characteristics on the parish/school web site with digital pictures of the individual leaders.

  (Make sure to obtain signed permission from each person's parents before posting photos on the Internet.)

MEDIA Youth Movies

MATERIALS NEEDED

TV/VCR

NOTES

- The service is an opportunity both to celebrate the current movies that tell the story of young people's lives and to challenge movie makers through prayer to portray young people on film as living lives of virtue and character.
- The Scripture readings set out examples of each of the four cardinal virtues. Each reading is followed immediately by a movie clip selected by the young people that demonstrates or opposes the same virtue.
- In preparation for this service, invite some of the young people to select two or three movie clips from their favorite current movies that either support or oppose the related virtue listed below.

GATHERING

- As part of the gathering and environment, preselect some movies that would be familiar to your group and create a ballot that addresses each of the four virtues ("Most Prudent Character," "Most Just Character," etc.), nominating characters for each category/virtue.
- Set up four voting stations and invite the young people to cast their ballots for each of the four categories/virtues.
- The voting results can be used in one of two ways: (1) The vote could determine which selection is shown during the prayer service, or (2) the group might discuss, as a third reflection question, how the winning selection does or does not represent the virtue in question.
- Play a variety of rhythmic songs of praise while the young people are gathering.

Suggested song:

I Will Praise Your Name (Bolduc)
Voices as One Hymnal #44, CD 2 Track 14.

Leader: In the name of the Father,
and of the Son,
and of the Holy Spirit.

All: Amen.

Leader:

Creating God,
we gather in the spirit of celebration
to praise you for the gifts of words, sounds,
and images
that help us live virtuously in our world.
We recall the stories of those
who chose prudence, justice,
fortitude, and temperance,
and we look to our own stories
in the movies that we share here
to learn how to write the next chapter
in the stories of our own lives.

45

Give us good judgment, just hearts,
brave souls, and balanced minds
as we praise your name
through the gifts of voice, movement, and pictures.
We ask this through Christ our Lord.

All: Amen.

Readings and Movie Clips

Prudence 1 Kings 3:4–12
         Movie Clip

Justice   John 8:2–11
         Movie Clip

Fortitude Ruth 1:15–18
         Movie Clip

Temperance Luke 6:27–31
          Movie Clip

TALKING POINTS

As you break open the Word, some points to share include:

- Solomon is mostly associated with the gift of wisdom. In our prayer, we focus on his ability to choose well when offered anything by God.
- God greatly rewards Solomon because of his virtuous, prudent choice, giving him everything that he could have asked for, but didn't.
- Jesus takes the Jewish notion of justice, especially in terms of enforcing the laws and their punishments, in a new direction in the story of the adulterous woman.
- Jesus reminds the townspeople that justice must be given out evenly.
- Ruth chooses to follow her mother-in-law, a woman who had no status in her world and a woman to whom she had no blood relationship.
- Ruth shows the fortitude or courage to make a difficult choice that is rooted in the love that she has for herself and for Naomi.
- Jesus proclaims in Luke that we love our enemy by resisting the natural, impulsive reactions that we often have—to hate or strike back—and names the ways in which we are called to respond.

REFLECTION

1. How do each of these movie clips portray the related virtue? In what ways do they reinforce or contradict the virtue?
2. What are the challenges that you face in trying to practice the virtue of prudence? Justice? Fortitude? Temperance?

Optional:
Invite the young people to write letters to the distributors, producers, directors, and writers of these movies to praise or critique them (as appropriate) for how they portray the ways in which young people deal with the four cardinal virtues and act virtuously in the movies' situations.

CLOSING

Leader:

Lord God,
you call us to live lives of virtue.
You give us models like Solomon, Ruth, and Jesus
to show us the way.
You give us examples in our movies
of virtue lived and virtue ignored.
Open our eyes, ears, hearts, and minds
so that we might become more prudent,
more just, more courageous, and more temperate
as we walk the pathway to our great reward
with you in the Kingdom of God.
We ask this through Christ our Lord.

All: Amen.

Suggested song:

I Will Praise Your Name (Bolduc)
Voices as One Hymnal #44, CD 2 Track 14

MEDIA Youth Music

MATERIALS NEEDED

Tape or CD player

NOTES

- This prayer service is a celebration of the music of young people, focusing on the theological virtues of faith, hope, and charity in a praise format.
- In preparation for the service, with the young people select the three pieces of music that correspond to the three theological virtues.
- At the heart of the praise portion of the service is the song *Come! Let Us Sing Out Our Praise!* (Tate). Invite your musically gifted young people to lead the music. Teach and practice the refrain of the song with the assembled before the gathering rite.

GATHERING

Leader: In the name of the Father,
and of the Son,
and of the Holy Spirit.

All: Amen.

Reading: Colossians 3:12–17

TALKING POINTS

As you break open the Word, some points to share include:

- Paul calls the community at Colossae to live virtuous lives, ultimately doing everything in the name of Jesus.
- We will focus on the three theological virtues, faith, hope, and charity (love). We practice the theological virtues as we try to grow closer to God, especially through Jesus.
- During this service, we do as Paul instructed—we give thanks and sing inspired songs to God in the name of Jesus, his Son.

Service of Praise and Thanksgiving Song:

Come! Let Us Sing Out Our Praise (Tate)
    Voices as One Hymnal #17, CD 1 Track 15

FAITH

Reading: Matthew 13:31–32
Song:
Contemporary song chosen by young people

Prayer

Leader:

> We thank you, Lord God,
> for by your goodness
> you have planted within our hearts
> the tiny seeds of faith.
> We sing out our praise to you
> with voices that acclaim your eternal wonder.

Response:

> *Come! Let Us Sing Out Our Praise* (Tate)
>   —Refrain only

HOPE

Reading: Romans 8:18–21, 24–25
Song:
Contemporary song chosen by young people

Prayer

Leader:

> We thank you, gracious God,
> for filling us with the hope
> of the glory of your Kingdom.
> As we patiently wait for that day,
> we give you praise and honor
> with the sound of joyful hearts.

Response:

> *Come! Let Us Sing Out Our Praise* (Tate)
>   —Refrain only

LOVE

Reading: 1 John 4:7–10
Song:
Contemporary song chosen by young people

Prayer

Leader:

> We thank you, God,
> for loving us
> so that through that love,
> we might come to know you
> through Your Son, Jesus Christ.
> With psalms, we sing you this inspired song
> of praise and gratitude.

Response:

> *Come! Let Us Sing Out Our Praise* (Tate)
>   —Refrain only

CLOSING

Invite the young people to respond spontaneously to the two parts of the prayer.

Leader:

For what do we thank God?

(Pause for responses)

For what do we praise God?

(Pause for responses)

> We praise you and thank you, Lord,
> with joyful hearts.
> May we live lives of faith, hope, and charity
> so that we may always be filled
> with the sounds of praise and thanksgiving.
> We ask this through your Son, Jesus,
> who is Lord forever and ever.

All: Amen.

Suggested songs include:

> *I Will Praise Your Name* (Bolduc)
>   Voices as One Hymnal #44, CD 2 Track 14
> *Lift Your Hearts to the Holy One* (Light/Tate)
>   Voices as One Hymnal #56, CD 3 Track 4

MEDIA Youth Videos

MATERIALS NEEDED

Video or slide show (see Notes)

NOTES

Before the service

- Invite a group of young people to create a music video/slide show using a video camera or still shots from a digital or 35mm camera.

- Suggested songs for the video/slide show are *He Is Jesus* (Bolduc) *Voices as One* Hymnal #34, CD 2 Track 6, or *On a Journey Together* (Angotti) *Voices as One* Hymnal #69, CD 3 Track 15. Other songs that focus on Jesus may be used. The lyrics should emphasize the core characteristics of Jesus and his ministry such as compassion, care, forgiveness, and faithfulness.

- The images might include young people from the class or youth group acting as Jesus did in the community.

After the service

- Plan a celebration at which videos of contemporary music may be shown (Christian and secular music).

GATHERING

Suggested song for the gathering is the song used for the video.

Leader: In the name of the Father,
and of the Son,
and of the Holy Spirit.

All: Amen.

Leader:

We gather today to celebrate the harmony
of words and actions,
to show how together they proclaim
God's saving word in Jesus.

Let us pray.

Creating God,
you spoke and the world was created.
You called and Abraham followed.
You whispered and Elijah heard you in the wind.
At his baptism, you named Jesus "your Son,"
and told us to listen to him.

Jesus' words spoke of freedom
from blindness and hunger,
from slavery and oppression,
from hatred and death.
Jesus put his own words into action
so that we might follow his way.

Keep your word in our mouths
so that we might always proclaim your greatness
in every word that we speak,
every song that we sing,
and every move that we make.

We ask this through Christ our Lord.

All: Amen.

Reading: Matthew 19:16–22

TALKING POINTS

As you break open the Word, some points to share include:

- Jesus tells the rich young man that he must sell all that he has in order to find perfection with God.
- This message stands in stark contrast to the message that we see in many music videos in which physical beauty, sexuality, and riches are seen as the way to happiness and fulfillment.
- The standard that Jesus sets out for us is himself—to do as he has done, to act as he has acted, to be like him.

REFLECTION

1. Which contemporary music video (Christian or secular music) presents the strongest message that goes against what Jesus asks of us? Give some examples from that video.
2. Which contemporary music video (Christian or secular music) presents the strongest message that supports what Jesus asks of us? Give some examples from that video.

Introduce the video or slide show that the youth created. Remind the young people that these are their own images of how they see Jesus acting through each other.

Play the video or slide show.

Prayers

Leader:

Our response is, "We thank you, Lord."

For your voice, which calls us to lives of love and compassion, mercy, and freedom.

Response…

For our voices, that we might proclaim your love and mercy among our friends and families and within our community.

Response…

For your Word, Jesus Christ, who has shown us how to love others as you have loved us.

Response…

For words, that we might use them to build up, not tear down, to comfort, not condemn, to bring peace, not violence.

Response…

For your way, which challenges us to give up all that we own and know in order to follow Jesus.

Response…

For the Way, that we might use the tools of technology to share the love of Jesus with others.

Response…

CLOSING

Leader:

Let us go forth and celebrate the presence of Jesus Christ in our lives.

Celebrate with a party featuring the videos of contemporary video music artists that continue to break open the Word of God and demonstrate who Jesus is in our lives.

Commitment to Preparation Process for Confirmation

MATERIALS NEEDED

Twigs or branches (about ½ to 1-inch in diameter)

Rocks and stones (palm-size and larger)

Fabric paint or permanent markers

Small grill for a fire (if possible)

Baskets for the rocks, stones, fabric paint, and markers

NOTES

- Designate an area at the front or center of the prayer space where the "fire" will be built. If it is possible to burn a small fire, place the grill there. If not, this will be the place where the twigs will be placed during the ritual portion of the service.
- Place the baskets of fabric paint or markers, rocks, and stones at the doorway of the prayer space.
- This prayer service works best if the chairs are removed from the prayer area so that the young people can sit on the floor.
- Before the service, take six to eight thinner branches (kindling) and write the key phrases from the readings below on them. These branches will be brought forward and arranged to form the basis of the "fire" during the reading section.
- Invite young people who are Boy Scouts, Girl Scouts, or Camp Fire members to help build the fire.
- Ask two or three young people (those who have already been confirmed would be ideal) prior to the prayer service to give a short witness on what particular story of Jesus has "burned in their hearts" and why.
- Place the larger twigs and branches in a pile(s) away from the "fire" area along with bottles of fabric paint or permanent markers.

GATHERING

- As the young people enter, invite them to take a rock or stone. Invite them to write on the stones the names of the people in whom they find their support, e.g., their family, friends, other concerned adults.
- Instruct the young people to take the rock or stone into the prayer space and place it in a ring around the outermost area of the prayer space so that all of the stones mark out the seating area for the prayer.

Call to Worship: Ezekiel 36:24–26

Leader: In the name of the Father,
and of the Son,
and of the Holy Spirit.

All: Amen.

Leader:

God of Fire,
we stand before you,
a community of young people,
preparing to enter the process
   that leads to the sacrament of Confirmation.

Take these hearts of ours,
turn their stoniness to openness,
and breathe into them the fire of your love
so that we may learn to live in the fullness
   of your Spirit
as we journey to Confirmation.

We ask this through Christ our Lord.

All: Amen.

Readings

This section is made up of multiple short readings on the images of heart and fire.

As the reader proclaims the reading, invite other members of the community to place the corresponding branches in the "fire" area (or give it to the young person who is helping create the basis for a fire.)

Reading 1:   Psalm 119:1–16

Reading 2:   Sirach 2:1–9

Reading 3:   Luke 24:32

TALKING POINTS

As you break open the Word, some points to share include:

- We use the image of fire because it is one of the traditional symbols of the Holy Spirit, the focus of Confirmation.
- We began our prayer with a reading from Ezekiel to remind us that at the start of the Confirmation process we must have open hearts. A fire can be built on stones, but not of stones.
- We wrote phrases from the readings on kindling, the narrow, driest wood, because kindling is the "starter" wood for all fires just as the Scripture is the starting point for our journey to the sacraments.
- Twigs and wood larger than kindling are the fuel for every fire, the fuel that makes it burn over time.
- As we came in, we wrote names on rocks and stones and placed them around us. In older, agrarian societies, rocks would have been used to mark out where the fire would be—much like a campfire today. The rocks also kept the fire from spreading and becoming destructive.
- The names of the people on the rocks and stones, like the members of this community, are the living stones that help make our hearts a place where the fire of and for Christ may dwell.
- Invite the two or three young people to share their reflections on the stories of Jesus that have "burned in their hearts."

RITUAL

Invite the young people to take the fabric paint or marker and write their answers to the following question on a twig or branch.

Who and what are the fuel for the fire to burn in your heart? Examples might include people in your life, certain significant experiences, books or songs, Bible stories.

Play quiet music in the background around the theme of the Holy Spirit (e.g., any version of *Veni Sancte Spiritus*).

As the young people finish writing, call out each person's name and invite them to come forward and share one of the answers that they wrote on their twig or branch and then place it on the "fire." Those who were helping previously could continue to help build the "fire."

Those who are candidates should sit around the "fire," forming a circle. Those who are not candidates (if any) should begin to form a circle around them like the ring of rocks and stones. They may sit or stand until everyone has come forward.

Leader:

Read the names of the candidates and ask them to stand at their places.

(To the candidates)

Do you present yourselves with open hearts to prepare to receive the sacrament of Confirmation?

Response: We do.

Are you ready to allow the stories of Jesus to burn in your hearts and call you forth to serve this community?

Response: We are.

Are you ready to kindle the fire of justice and peace, of love and understanding, of wisdom and gratitude so that it may burn within you?

Response: We are.

Invite the rest of the community to stand at their places.

(To the rest of the community)

Are you willing to be the living stones that surround and support these candidates as they kindle the fire of the Holy Spirit in preparation for the sacrament of Confirmation?

Response: We are.

Candidates, you have declared your commitment to prepare for the sacrament of Confirmation. Community of
_____,
(name of parish or school)
you have declared your commitment to support these candidates in their continuing faith journey.

Until we gather to celebrate the sacrament
   of Confirmation,
may we walk in faith, fueled by the stories
   of Jesus' love and salvation,
with hearts that burn to proclaim
that Jesus is Lord in every word we speak
and everything we do.
We ask this in his name
   who is Lord for ever and ever.

All: Amen.

CLOSING

Suggested songs include:

Great One in Three (Tate/Berrell)
   Voices as One Hymnal #30, CD 2 Track 3
Lay Down That Spirit (Mattingly)
   Voices as One Hymnal #52, CD 3 Track 1

Death of a Classmate

MATERIALS NEEDED

Tissues
Cross
Paschal candle
Bowl of holy water
Small bowl of oil or the container of chrism
Eucharistic bread and cup or bottle of wine
Baptismal candle (of the deceased, if possible)
Objects belonging to the deceased

NOTES

- Create an atmosphere of support by inviting older peers, adults, or parish/school staff members to welcome the participants.
- Promote listening skills among the young people and encourage them to tell stories about their classmate during the prayer service.
- Invite counselors and trusted adults as participants to model strong listening skills.
- Emphasize that it is important that we gather as a community to pray about the classmate's death rather than separating ourselves and being alone during this time.
- Place the cross, paschal candle, baptismal candle, water, oil, bread, and wine at the front or in the center of the prayer space in an attractive grouping.
- Select a number of friends and peers to participate in the opening process.
- Before the service select two or three good friends of the deceased who would be willing to share a particular memory or story about their classmate.

GATHERING

- Invite a leader to remind the community why they are gathering and who it is they are remembering.
- Light the paschal candle, then the baptismal candle from it.
- Process in with the objects and place them around the cross and candles.

Suggested song during this procession:

In the Light (Poirier)
Voices as One Hymnal #48, CD 2 Track 18

First Reading: Luke 24:13–24

TALKING POINTS

As you break open the Word, some points to share include:

- The story of Cleopas and his friend reminds us that grief is natural and that it is experienced in a variety of ways.
- At this time, it is important for us to honor whatever we are experiencing and to allow ourselves to feel our grief just as Cleopas and his friend did.
- Cleopas and his friend were only two of many people grieving for Jesus' death. Their disappointment challenged their faith in Jesus as the Messiah—this was a crisis of faith for them.

REFLECTION

1. Put yourself in the place of Cleopas. How would you have felt? What would you be thinking? How would you react to this stranger, especially his ignorance about Jesus and the recent events in Jerusalem?
2. How might the other followers—the eleven apostles, the other disciples, Mary and the women, those he healed—be reacting now?
3. Putting yourself in the shoes of any of Jesus' followers, what would be your most significant story about Jesus to share with others?

Second Reading: Luke 24:25–35

TALKING POINTS

As you break open the Word, some points to share include:

- Jesus reminded his companions of the importance of remembering, telling stories about him.
- Jesus also reminded them that death is a part of life.
- It was only when they were able to reconnect to their experiences of Jesus that they recognized Jesus among them. As we know, they recognized Jesus in the actions that were most closely identified with him.
- Once they reconnected to their faith in him, their inability to recognize him was lifted. We need faith to provide us the light to see the presence of Christ in each other and in the world.
- We have these objects as reminders of the deceased, but they can't shout, cry, sing, or speak about the person he/she was, so we must.

REFLECTION

In pairs, tell a story about the person who has died. Feel free to use the objects as a point of reference for your sharing.

As a large group, share some of the key characteristics of the person who died that emerged from the stories that were told.

Invite the two or three young people to come forward to share their story of the deceased.

Intercessions

> Response: Lord, hear our prayer

For _____, our friend, classmate, and companion in faith.
We pray to the Lord . . .

For _____'s family as they grieve.
We pray to the Lord . . .

For all of those who have died,
especially our friends, family members, and
_____ (names of people from the parish or school community.)
We pray to the Lord . . .

For what else would we like to pray . . .
(Allow a short pause for people to share their own intentions.)
We pray to the Lord . . .

Our Father

Invite the participants to join hands if that is the local custom.

CLOSING

Leader:

> Let us leave, as Cleopas and his companion did, to continue our journey
>   to the heavenly Jerusalem,
> sharing the stories of our friend
> _____.
>
> May _____ have everlasting life with God.
>
> We ask this through Christ our Lord.

All: Amen.

Suggested songs include:

Journey for Home (Bolduc)
    Voices as One Hymnal #50, CD 2 Track 20

On a Journey Together (Angotti)
    Voices as One Hymnal #69, CD 3 Track 15

DRIVING
Blessing of Driver's Licenses & Keys

MATERIALS NEEDED

Bible

Prayer table with appropriate cloth

Paschal candle placed near the table

Token fob to give to each new driver with the name or symbol of the parish—something to put on their keychain (if possible).

NOTES

- Other friends and family members can be invited to this service.
- Ask the new drivers to place their licenses and keys on the prayer table before the service.
- Set up the prayer table at the front or in the center of the prayer space.

GATHERING

As people are gathering, the group might sing. Suggested selections include:

Come, Christians, Unite (Bolduc)
   Voices as One Hymnal #15, CD 1 Track 13

Come! Let Us Sing Out Our Praise (Tate)
   Voices as One Hymnal #17, CD 1 Track 15

Glorify the Lord with Me (Tate)
   Voices as One Hymnal #24, CD 1 Track 20

Here I Am, O God (Warner)
   Voices as One Hymnal #36, CD 2 Track 8

I Choose You (Cooney)
   Voices as One Hymnal #40, CD 2 Track 10

I Will Praise Your Name (Bolduc)
   Voices as One Hymnal #44, CD 2 Track 14

Leader: In the name of the Father, and of the Son, and of the Holy Spirit.

All: Amen.

Reading: Exodus 13:17–22

TALKING POINTS

As you break open the Word, some points to share include:

- God led the Hebrews out of Egypt in a roundabout way, away from danger and fighting, to remind them to take courage in their journey.
- Driving can be dangerous and scary, especially for new drivers who are still learning to be comfortable on the road.
- As new drivers, it takes courage each time you get in the car to be safe and act responsibly.
- The Hebrews are a good model of safety and responsibility.
- They left Egypt fully armed to protect themselves, and they remembered to take Joseph's bones with them because they were certain that God would visit them. That was their commitment to God.

- God stayed with the Israelites, preceding them as a cloud by day and a column of fire by night. God promised to stay with them and guide them, and God did.
- As you begin your journey, you are well equipped, not with weapons and bones, but with knowledge and skills.

RITUAL

Invite the new drivers to stand at their places.

Leader:
Today/tonight we celebrate your arrival at a new destination in your life journey—receiving your driver's license. We gather as the faith community of _____ to rejoice and support you as you begin driving. The state of _____ has certified that you meet its requirements and have demonstrated the ability to drive. This community now asks you to declare your commitment to serve God and the community with this new-found responsibility in the presence of your peers.

(Response is "I will.")

Leader: Each time you drive,
will you equip yourselves
with the knowledge and skills
that you have learned?

Response: I will.

Leader: Each time you drive,
will you be models of safety
and responsible action?

Response: I will.

Leader: Each time you drive,
will you be faithful to what God
asks of you—to keep the laws,
to show kindness and mercy,
to trust in God?

Response: I will.

Leader: *(Ask the rest of the community to stand)*
As a community of faith,
will you commit yourselves
to supporting these new drivers?

Response: We will.

- Leader holds up keychain fob and explains to the new drivers that this is a sign of the community's commitment to support them. Encourage them to put it on their keychain as a reminder.
- Invite one or two of the young people to pass out one of the keychain fobs to each new driver.
- Invite members of the community to go to the table and pick up the license and keys of one driver and put them in the outstretched hands of the new driver.
- Ask one person to put their hands over the new driver's hands.
- Invite the rest of the community to cluster around a new driver and put their hand on the shoulder of the new driver.

Leader:
God of signs and wonders,
   in ancient times
you showed yourself as a cloud by day
   and fire by night
to guide the Israelites' way to their promised home.
Be with these new drivers
   throughout their journeys.
Bless and protect them on the roads.
May this license be a reminder of their call
   to be safe and responsible drivers.
May these keys be used wisely as they journey
   through many adventures.
May this community of faith
   continue to support these new drivers
   through prayer and constant vigilance.
We ask this through your Son, Jesus Christ,
   who is Lord for ever and ever.

All: Amen.

Ring the keys.

CLOSING SONG

Suggested songs include:
Come, Christians, Unite (Bolduc)
   Voices as One Hymnal #15, CD 1 Track 13
Glorify the Lord with Me (Tate)
   Voices as One Hymnal #24, CD 1 Track 20
I Choose You (Cooney)
   Voices as One Hymnal #40, CD 2 Track 10
I Have Been Anointed (Warner)
   Voices as One Hymnal #42, CD 2 Track 12
Lift Your Hearts to the Holy One (Light/Tate)
   Voices as One Hymnal #56, CD 3 Track 4
Show Us the Way (Light/Tate)
   Voices as One Hymnal #83, CD 4 Track 5

INITIATION
Entering the Initiation Process

MATERIALS NEEDED

Butcher paper
Tape
Pens
Markers
Cross
Holy water
Chrism oil (if available)
Bread and wine

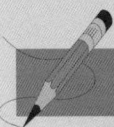

NOTES

- This service assumes that the catechumens and candidates have already celebrated the Rite of Acceptance into the Order of Catechumens and/or the Rite of Welcoming the Candidates. The questions that are part of the commitment prayer are similar to some of the questions asked during those rites and are intended only as a reminder.
- Select an area at the front or center of the prayer space and arrange the cross, holy water, chrism, and bread and wine in such a way that everyone will be able to see the symbols of initiation.
- Cut the paper into various lengths and tape them together to form a "winding" road. (See notes below to determine how many taped lengths are needed.) Turns in this road can range from subtle to hairpin. The shape of the road should be creative and unpredictable.
- If the cross and other symbols are placed at the front of the room, make one road by taping all of the lengths together and laying it on the floor, starting at the doorway where people will enter and ending where the cross, holy water, chrism, and bread and wine are placed.

GATHERING

Suggested songs include:

Glorify the Lord with Me (Tate)
   Voices as One Hymnal #24, CD 1 Track 20
He Is Jesus (Bolduc)
   Voices as One Hymnal #34, CD 2 Track 6

Leader: In the name of the Father,
          and of the Son,
          and of the Holy Spirit.

All: Amen.

Leader:

Lord Jesus Christ,
by the sign of your cross,
you set us free from death
and brought us into new life with you.

- If the cross and other symbols are at the center of the room, cut the paper into multiple lengths that include smaller curves and place them like rays of the sun, starting from the outermost edge of the room and leading toward the symbols.
- On the paper, write in larger letters the following words: "Baptism" towards the starting end, "Confirmation" about one-third of the way down the paper, and "Eucharist" about two-thirds of the way down the paper.
- Invite several young people to lead the welcoming as everyone gathers. Try to create a strong atmosphere of hospitality for this service.
- As the young people gather, ask them to sit around the paper, not on it, near the end(s) closest to the door or walls.

58

We gather together
as a pilgrim people,
journeying toward the fullness of your kingdom
when it comes.

Among us are _____
(names of catechumens/candidates).

We join them on the path as they enter
the process that leads to the sacraments
of initiation.

Lead us and guide us
that we may walk in your ways,
and come to know the new life
to which you have called us.

You are Lord and Savior, for ever and ever.

All: Amen.

First Reading: 1 Corinthians 13:11

TALKING POINTS

As you break open the Word, some points to share include:

- This reading is one verse from Paul's famous letter to the Corinthians in which he talks about love and how our experiences and perceptions of love change as we grow older and wiser.
- The journey of faith is a journey of love—the love of God—and, as the verse indicates, our experience of love and faith changes as we grow older.
- As we begin our reflection, we will examine how our faith and love of God have changed as we have come to know God and Jesus.

RITUAL

The butcher paper represents the journey of faith with its many turns.

The journey begins at the doorway of our birth and leads to the water, oil, bread, and wine of initiation, and ultimately to the cross and resurrection of Jesus.

On the edges of the paper, in the space around the word "Baptism" and before the word "Confirmation," invite the young people to write or draw their answers to the following questions. The answers can be in words or pictures.

1. What were the first things that you believed about God when you were a young child?
2. What experiences, people, activities helped support your faith?
3. How would you have described God?
4. With two or three people nearby, invite them to share their responses to these questions.

Play the song *The Face of God* (Bolduc)
Voices as One Hymnal #88, CD 4 Track 9.

At the end of the song, invite the young people to move to the section of the paper between the words "Confirmation" and "Eucharist."

Ask them to write or draw their answers to the following questions.

1. What do you know and believe about God now that you didn't know and believe when you were younger?
2. Where do you see the face of God or the face of Jesus in your life now?

In the large group, ask some of the young people to share their responses to both of these questions.

When the sharing is completed, invite the young people to move all the way to the front or center.

Second Reading: Romans 6:3–11

TALKING POINTS

As you break open the Word, some points to share include:

- This is the New Testament reading for the Easter Vigil.
- Paul writes about how our membership in the community of Jesus Christ is nothing like belonging to a club. It is membership and participation in Jesus' death and the new life of the Resurrection.
- We mark various points in our faith journey with sacraments, but the journey of faith never ends.
- We continue to experience Jesus' death and resurrection throughout our life-long journey.
- Along this journey, we walk with other members of our faith community.

Prayer of Commitment

To the catechumens and candidates:

Leader:

You have presented yourselves to the Catholic community of _____,
(name of parish or school).
What do ask of the Church?

Catechumens/candidates may respond in their own words or the group may decide on one response to be said together (some answers include faith, initiation, a specific sacrament).

Will you carefully study the Scripture and traditions of the Church?

Response: We will (or "Yes").

Will you open yourselves to sharing in the stories of this faith community as you journey toward Easter?

Response: We will (or "Yes").

To their companions:

Leader:

These catechumens (and candidates) have presented themselves to this Catholic community, and are prepared to enter into the journey that leads to full initiation.

Will you serve as guides and mentors, helping to break open the word and model the Catholic life, as these young people study Scripture and the traditions of the Church?

Response: We will (or "Yes").

Will you share the stories of your faith journey with these catechumens (and candidates) as they journey toward Easter?

Response: We will (or "Yes").

To all:

Leader:

Will you journey together to the great sacraments of Easter as companions in Christ Jesus?

Response: We will (or "Yes").

May our Lord Jesus Christ
be our strength for this journey.

Song:

Strength for the Journey (Poirier)
   Voices as One Hymnal #87, CD 4 Track 8

Encourage the young people to sing the refrain.

Leader:

We are sent forth
to be strength for each other
on the journey to the saving waters of Baptism,
the sealing oil of Confirmation,
and the living bread and wine of Eucharist.

May our catechumens (and candidates)
discover the freedom from sin and death
that comes in living the death and resurrection
   of Jesus Christ.

May we as companions remember and live anew
the life in Christ that was given to us
in our initiation.

We ask this in the name of Jesus Christ,
who is Lord for ever and ever.

All: Amen.

CLOSING

Suggested songs include:

On a Journey Together (Angotti)
   Voices as One Hymnal #69, CD 3 Track 15
Show Us the Way (Light/Tate)
   Voices as One Hymnal #83, CD 4 Track 5
Walk in the Land (Mattingly)
   Voices as One Hymnal #94, CD 4 Track 14
We Will Walk (Bolduc)
   Voices as One Hymnal #102, CD 4 Track 21

Forgiveness

MATERIALS NEEDED

Paschal candle (or one or more tall candles)
Fireproof bowl or canister lined with sand
Small table or stack of fireproof bricks or stones
Matches
Small slips of paper
Pens or pencils
Pail of water or sand or a fire extinguisher

NOTES

- At the center of the space, place the table or stack of fireproof bricks or stones. Put the fireproof bowl or canister on the table or bricks/stones.
- Place the paschal candle next to the bowl or canister. Make sure that the participants will be able to reach the lit wick of the candle.
- Set up a ring of chairs, one per person, facing outward away from the center. If there are many people, position chairs facing outward radiating away from the center of the space. The most important thing is that, when seated, people cannot see the face of another person.
- Place a slip of paper and a pen or pencil near each chair.
- Because the slips of paper will be burned during the prayer service, keep a pail of water or sand or a fire extinguisher under the table or nearby.
- This service focuses on recognizing how sin divides us in our relationships with God, others, and ourselves and explores two of the four elements of sacramental reconciliation: contrition and confession.
- Contrition includes the experience of *metanoia*, a "turning around." The young people will physically turn their seats around as a symbol of their turning from the darkness of sin to the light of Christ.

GATHERING

- As the young people arrive, ask them to find a seat and sit in silence.
- The silence is intended as an aural symbol of isolation and separation during the gathering, so no music is recommended.

Reading: John 8:2–11

TALKING POINTS

As you break open the Word, some points to share include:

- Sin causes separation in our relationships with God, others, and ourselves.
- The adulteress was guilty of sin in all three of its dimensions.
- Her adultery broke God's law and her relationship with God. Her adultery, by definition, caused a break in the relationship between other people. Her adultery also isolated her from the goodness within her, the goodness given to all of us by God.
- Though this sin was against one of the Ten Commandments, Jesus forgives her.
- Early Christians called adultery a mortal sin, the worst type of sin.
- Jesus demonstrates through his own compassion and mercy the degree to which God forgives us—and the degree to which God expects us to forgive others and ourselves.
- The paschal candle is our constant reminder that Jesus saved us from sin through his death and resurrection, and that we are called to die to our sins on a regular basis so that we might live more fully with him.

- Remind the young people when the service is scheduled or at the end of the service that they have not participated in the sacrament of Reconciliation. As a next step after this service, encourage them to participate in the sacrament at the next available opportunity.

RITUAL

In silence, invite the young people to think of something they have said or done (or something they haven't said or haven't done)—a sin—that has created a separation in any relationship in their life.

Ask them to write what was said or done on the slip of paper.

One by one, invite them to come to the center and burn the slip of paper in the bowl or canister. When they return to their seat, ask them to turn their chair so that it is facing the center.

Note: This is most effective when the young people come forward one at a time. Because they cannot see each other, remind them to use their other senses, especially hearing and smell, to determine when to get up and when to wait.

REFLECTION

Reading: Ephesians 5:8–14

Invite the young people to reflect on the following questions and share their responses with a partner.

1. What did it feel like to enter this room in silence and sit without seeing anyone's face?
2. In what ways was your experience of silence and isolation in this room similar to your sin in the relationship that you wrote about and burned in the fire?
3. How did your sin make you feel about yourself? About God? About the other person?
4. What stood (or stands) in your way of asking for forgiveness and bringing healing to that relationship?
5. What could you do to ask for forgiveness and begin healing that relationship?

Intercessions

Leader:

> As a community,
> we have begun our prayer
> of healing and reconciliation
> with God, others, and ourselves.
>
> We turn to God now,
> the healer of all of the world's pain and sin,
> and raise our prayers to the Lord.
>
> Let our response be: Lord, have mercy on us.

> For the places in our world that are ravaged by war and violence, especially _____ , that they may know peace.
> We pray to the Lord . . .
>
> For the leaders of our communities, that their hearts may be open to finding ways to bring healing to our cities, neighborhoods, and schools.
> We pray to the Lord . . .
>
> For our church leaders, especially Pope _____ and (Arch)Bishop _____ , that they may continue to faithfully preach the Gospel of repentance and live God's mercy.
> We pray to the Lord . . .
>
> For our families and friends who help us build God's kingdom of justice and peace.
> We pray to the Lord . . .
>
> For this community gathered in faith, seeking forgiveness and witnessing to the power of God's mercy and love.
> We pray to the Lord…

Invite the young people to offer their prayers aloud.

Our Father

Leader:

> Jesus taught us to forgive those
>   who sin against us.
> Let us pray in the words Jesus gave us.
> Our Father…

Sign of Peace

Leader:

> In a spirit of peace and forgiveness,
> let us offer each other a sign of peace.

CLOSING

Suggested song:

In the Light (Poirier)
  Voices as One Hymnal #48, CD 2 Track 18

SERVICE
Blessing of Objects Used in Service Projects

MATERIALS NEEDED

Objects for service projects, e.g., hammers, nails, food, clothing—there should be sufficient quantities of these objects so that each participant can carry an item in the opening procession

Holy water and bowl (if desired, the water can be blessed by a priest or deacon as a part of this prayer service)

NOTES

- This prayer service assumes that the service opportunities for the young people are in the local community.
- Place the bowl of blessed water on a table at the front or in the center of the prayer space.

GATHERING

- Invite the young people to process in with an object for a service project. Encourage them to raise the objects high (shoulder height) as they walk with them to the front or center of the prayer space.
- Designate one or two young people or adults to receive the objects and assist the young people in placing them around the bowl of water.

Suggested song to be played and sung during the procession:

I Have Been Anointed (Warner)
   Voices as One Hymnal #42, CD 2 Track 12

Readings   Luke 4:16–22
            John 13:12–15

TALKING POINTS

As you break open the Word, some points to share include:

- In Jesus' reading from the prophet Isaiah, we hear the simple statement of how and for whom Jesus intends to live his life and ministry.
- Jesus' washing of the feet of his apostles is the primary example that we have of service.
- Jesus takes ordinary objects, like water and a towel, and through his actions with them transforms them into symbols of service.
- He also takes a daily ritual of foot-washing—something that would be done by the lowliest of servants—and demonstrates how the simplest, most common action can become a manifestation of God's presence in the world.
- Together, Jesus' words "As I have done, so you must do" in John and his proclamation in Luke tell us how we are to serve and how we are to use the gifts that God has given us in service to others.

RITUAL

- Invite a variety of people from the gathered community to sprinkle water on the objects around the table. It is important that they use their hands.
- If the community is not gathered around the objects or near them, invite them to come forward if space allows.
- Ask everyone to raise their hands in blessing over the objects.

Leader:

Loving God,
you set an example of service through the life of your Son, Jesus Christ.

He taught us how to build up your kingdom,
how to nurture love for you and our neighbor,
how to be clothed and to clothe others
in your compassion.

We ask that you bless these
_____ (name the objects).

May they be our simple instruments of service as we go forth to do as Jesus did.

We ask this in Jesus' name,
who is Lord for ever and ever.

All: Amen.

Intercessions

Response: Lord, hear our prayer.

For those who serve the poor and the hungry, the blind and the lame, and the prisoners and the oppressed, we pray to the Lord . . .

For those in need, that we may hear their call and respond as Jesus did, we pray to the Lord . .

For those who control the resources needed by others, that they may be generous and act justly as they share those resources, we pray to the Lord . . .

For _____ (name the specific service activities for which the objects will be used), we pray to the Lord . . .

We make our prayer
through Christ our Lord.

All: Amen.

CLOSING

Leader:

We leave this place to serve as Jesus did.

May we live our "Amen" as we use these objects to continue to build God's Kingdom.

Invite the participants to process the objects to their final "resting place," e.g., boxes for transport, trunk of a car.

Suggested songs include:

I Have Been Anointed (Warner)
    Voices as One Hymnal #42, CD 2 Track 12

Show Us the Way (Light/Tate)
    Voices as One Hymnal #83, CD 4 Track 5

SERVICE
Blessing of Hands for Christian Service

MATERIALS NEEDED

Tape (masking, bandage)
Large bowl of salt water
Small bowl of mud or ashes
Small bowl of unblessed, scented oil

NOTES

- Arrange a table at the front or center of the prayer space with the bowls of mud or ashes, water, and oil. During the signing, young people will come forward to each station, starting with the mud or ashes, then the water, then the oil.
- Identify three people (adults or young people) to assist with the signing. The signers with mud or ashes and oil will be able to hold their bowl. The signer with the water may want to leave the bowl on the table.
- As people are arriving, tape their hands into fists with masking or bandage tape so that they cannot open them.

GATHERING

- Invite everyone to welcome each other with a greeting. Allow this to be a little silly.
- Ask everyone to stand in a circle, if possible, with their fists extended.

Call to Worship: Ezekiel 36:26

Leader:

These are hard hands,
hands ready for defiance,
for hatred, for violence,
for destruction, and for war.

These hands show no mercy.

These clenched fists cannot welcome the poor,
the oppressed, the imprisoned, the hurting.

Ask two or three of the adults or young people to cut open the tape so that the participants can remove the tape from their hands.

Ask everyone to open their hands with the palms up.

These are open hands,
welcoming hands,
hands of humility and compassion,
hands of love and service.

We thank you, Lord, for these open hands.
Let us welcome each other with open hands,
open arms, and open hearts.

Invite the young people to greet each other with a sign of welcome—a handshake or a hug.

Reading: Matthew 12:9–13

TALKING POINTS

As you break open the Word, some points to share include:

- The purpose of this healing is to demonstrate to the Pharisees that good deeds may be performed on the Sabbath though the law strictly forbade this.
- Jesus uses a hypothetical situation, "Suppose you lose a sheep …" to try to help the Pharisees understand why this healing is permissible.
- In the hypothetical situation, the sheep owner would need to use his hands in order to rescue his errant sheep.
- The man with the shriveled hand was impeded from performing any act of service that would require the use of that hand.
- As we know from other Gospel stories about Jesus, serving God by serving others was at the center of Jesus' ministry, regardless of the particular day the acts of service were done.
- By healing the man's hand, Jesus freed the man from the physical binding that had prevented him from serving others with that hand.

REFLECTION

1. Close your hand and make a fist. As you look at your fist, name the times in your life when you have closed your fist or used your fist. Why did you close your fist? Share your reflections with two other people.
2. With your fist still closed, name the things that you cannot do with a closed hand. How would life be different if you could not do those things?
3. Open your fist now. What are three activities or actions that you can do because you can open your hand? Why are they important to you?

RITUAL

Ask the adults or young people who will be the signers to come forward and pick up their bowls.

Explain the symbolism of each bowl.

- The mud or ashes remind us of our humanity, the many needs of the earth, and the sometimes difficult call to serve.
- The salt water reminds us of the tears and sweat that we often experience when we serve others—tears of frustration, sadness, anger, joy; the sweat of hard work.
- The oil is the Church's symbol of service, of our anointing to be priests and prophets in our world.

Invite each young person to come to each of the signers, starting with the mud or ashes. Each signer should trace the sign of the cross on the palm of the young person's hand.

The water signer may dip the young person's hand underwater and as he/she is tracing the sign of the cross, wipe away some of the mud or ashes. Because the water is symbolic of some of the grittiness of service, letting the water get muddy is allowable. The young people proceed to the signer with oil.

- As they are signing, the signers say, "These are hands of Christ. These are hands of service."
- Instrumental or vocal music can be played in the background.

Suggested songs include:

Christ, Be Near at Either Hand (arr. Gillen)
   Voices as One Hymnal #14, CD 1 Track 12

If Today You Hear the Voice of God (Bolduc)
   Voices as One Hymnal #45, CD 2 Track 15

CLOSING

Ask the young people to extend their hands, palms up.

Leader:
   Lord,
   these are hard-working hands,
   hands ready for service,
   for love, for compassion,
   for building, and for peace.
   These are hands of mercy.
   These open hands are ready to welcome the poor,
   the oppressed, the imprisoned, the hurt.
   We ask you to bless these hands.
   May they embrace you in the faces, hands, and hearts of everyone we meet as we go forth to serve you.
   We ask this through your Son Jesus,
   who is Lord for ever and ever.

All: Amen.

Suggested song:

I Have Been Anointed (Warner)
   Voices as One Hymnal #42, CD 2 Track 12

Violence Within the Local Community

MATERIALS NEEDED

Pieces of foamcore cut into 24 x 30-inch pieces, one piece for each two to three people

Pens or markers

Cross

Candles or luminaria

NOTES

- It is important to emphasize the experience of being a community rather than being alone during this time.
- Create a "safe" space for prayer.
- *Suggestions include:*
  - Placing a cross at the center or front of the space.
  - Encircling the space with candles or luminaria.
- Before the prayer service, select any number of quotes from the Book of Psalms listed below. These particular psalms express a variety of emotions. Write the quotes on the foamcore, allowing sufficient room for the young people to write on the foamcore later in the service.
- Place pieces of foamcore and markers or pens around the room, near the candles.
- During the prayer service, it is important that the young people feel listened to, that they have an opportunity to "sound off," and that they know that they are supported by everyone present as they deal with their response to the situation.

7:2	33:20	55:2	116:1–2
10:1	33:22	61:2	120:16
10:12	35:17–18	62:2	121:16
12:8	40:2	70:2	125:1b
13:2	42:10	71:1	130:1b
3:4	43:2	74:16	141:10
16:16	52:7	83:2	143:1b
17:16	53:2a	94:1	
18:2–3	54:4	102:2–3	

GATHERING

- As the young people enter, invite them to read the psalm quotes on the various pieces of foamcore and ask them to find one that has meaning for them.
- Play soft instrumental music as they gather.

Leader:

As you entered this room,
we invited you to find a quote from the
Book of Psalms that has meaning
for you right now.

We gather today to reflect on

_____

(describe the incident of violence that prompted this prayer service).

The cross reminds us that our safety
  is in its shadow,
and our candles recall that Christ is the light
  in whom there is no darkness.

We gather in the name of the one
  who knew violence in his death
  and rose to new life
so that we might never be left in the darkness
  of despair, pain, anger, and sorrow.

In the name of the Father,
and of the Son,
and of the Holy Spirit.

All: Amen.

Reading, Part 1:   Psalm 77:2–13

TALKING POINTS

As you break open the Word, some points to share include:

- The psalms are the voice of people who loved their God and brought all of their concerns to the Lord, including their anger and pain.
- The psalmist reminds us that God expects and even desires that we bring God the variety of emotions and responses we are experiencing at this time.

RITUAL

- The foamcore will serve as the young people's "sounding board," a way to address their thoughts, feelings, concerns, and questions to God.
- Invite the young people to write what they want to say to God about this experience of violence on that piece of foamcore.
- Play as much music as is needed to cover the reflection time.

Suggested songs includes:

Answer When I Call (Tate)
   Voices as One Hymnal #3, CD 1 Track 3

Crux Fidelis (Warner)
   Voices as One Hymnal #19, CD 1 Track 16

He Answers All Our Needs (Bolduc)
   Voices as One Hymnal #33, CD 2 Track 5

Hear Me, O God (Tate)
   Voices as One Hymnal #35, CD 2 Track 7

- Invite them to share what they wrote or why they selected the quote from Psalms with two or three people around them. The following questions might direct the conversation.
- What have been some of my emotional responses to this experience of violence? My physical responses? My spiritual responses?
- How has this experience of violence affected my perception of who God is? My faith and confidence in God?
- Ask the small groups to share some of their thoughts, feelings, and responses with the large group. Encourage them to talk about their experience in the first person (sometimes teens gravitate toward using second-person language unconsciously —"You feel …").

Reading, Part 2:   Psalm 77:14–21

TALKING POINT

As you break open the Word, one point to share is:

- One of the characteristics of psalms like this one is that the psalmist always ends by telling God that he has confidence and hope in God.

REFLECTION

Invite the young people to share their responses to the following question in the same small groups.

1. What would it take for me to have hope like the psalmist does in response to this experience in our community?

- Invite each group to take their piece of foamcore and process with it up to the cross and to sit close to the cross. Remind them that this is our symbolic way of bringing our experience of this violent incident to Jesus.
- During the procession, play any of the songs listed at left.

Reading, Part 3:   Romans 5:1–11

TALKING POINTS

As you break open the Word, some points to share include:

- Paul reminds us that the response to all afflictions is hope.
- Paul trusts that despite whatever we might experience, we are saved by the once and forever death and resurrection of Jesus—that because of the cross, we never need lose hope.
- We are encouraged to bring all of our pains and sorrows to the cross of Jesus, where we know by faith that our pains and sorrows will be borne by him.

Intercessions

Sung refrain: *Answer Me* (Bolduc)
   Voices as One Hymnal #4, CD 1 Track 4

For those who experience violence, especially _____ (name the incident[s] for which the group is gathered). We pray to the Lord …

Refrain: *Answer Me* (Bolduc)

For those who perform acts of violence—
physical, emotional, spiritual violence.
We pray to the Lord . . .

Refrain: Answer Me (Bolduc)

For the families and friends of those who experience violence, that they may create safe havens of love and peace.
We pray to the Lord . . .

Refrain: Answer Me (Bolduc)

For this faith community of _____ (name of parish or school), that we may bear the pain and sorrow of those around us and boast of our hope in Christ Jesus.
We pray to the Lord . . .

Refrain: Answer Me (Bolduc)

CLOSING

Our Father . . .

Sign of Peace

Suggested song:

In You, O Lord (Bolduc)
Voices as One Hymnal #49, CD 2 Track 19

Violence Outside the Local Community

MATERIALS NEEDED

Foamcore cut into pieces the size of bricks

Markers

"Blessed are the Peacemaker" buttons and 800-cards (can be purchased from the National Federation for Catholic Youth Ministry) or another token that focuses on peacemaking

NOTES

- During this prayer service, we want to break down symbolically the walls of violence that isolate and divide us in order to build paths of peace.

- Invite a group of young people to mime the behaviors that Jesus suggests during the first part of the reading (Luke 6:27–30).

- Invite a few young people to be prepared to describe the experiences of violence that have brought the community together.

- In preparation for the service, build a wall of the foamcore bricks, stacking them like a house of cards. The wall does not need to be tall nor very stable.

GATHERING

Begin by asking the young people to share the experiences of violence that are the focus of this prayer service.

Leader: In the name of the Father,
and of the Son,
and of the Holy Spirit.

All: Amen.

Leader:

God of bricks and stones,
you called us to be builders,
to build homes and cities,
to build walls and bridges,
to build love and peace.

Sometimes our homes and cities are divided
by walls of violence
built by the hands of many,
some through action,
some through inaction.

You called us to be builders,
not dividers.

May we come to know how to turn
the bricks and stones for building
from walls of hatred and violence
to pathways of love and peace.
We ask this through Christ our Lord.

All: Amen.

Reading: Luke 6:27–36

TALKING POINTS

As you break open the Word, some points to share include:

- Walls are often built to protect us, but they also divide us, separating us from the "evil," the "bad," the "other" that is outside.
- Walls can be material and physical or emotional and spiritual.
- All walls create a sense of "us/them"—a sense of rivals or opponents.
- Acts of violence create or reinforce all types of walls and isolate us from one another.
- Jesus calls us to take action to break down the walls of violence and build pathways to peace.
- By each action that we take, even the smallest action, we can break down the walls.

RITUAL

What concrete actions can you take to bring peace to this community, to our society, to our world?

- One by one, invite the young people to come forward and take a brick. The wall will eventually tumble.
- On the brick, ask them to write the one action to which they would be willing to commit.
- On the reverse side, ask the young people to write their own prayer for peace.
- Invite the young people to come forward and, with their bricks, build a road of peace. As they place their bricks, ask them to read their action.

Intercessions

Leader:

We have been called by God
to be builders of peace.

Now we call upon our God
to hear our prayers for peace.

Let our response be: Lord, be our peace.

For violence in our homes, our schools,
our workplaces, and our neighborhoods,
we pray to the Lord . . .

For _____,
(the reason for the prayer service)
we pray to the Lord . . .

For an end to hunger, thirst, homelessness,
and poverty, some of the reasons that violence
in our world occurs,
we pray to the Lord . . .

For those who suffer the scars and ravages
of violence, that God may heal their hearts,
minds, and bodies,
we pray to the Lord . . .

For those who participate in violence
in any form and those who provide the means
to support violence, that they may put down
their weapons and hear the call of the Lord
to lasting peace,
we pray to the Lord . . .

For those who strive to build pathways of peace,
that each act of love and understanding may
bring the peace of God closer to reality,
we pray to the Lord . . .

Blessed are the peacemakers,
for they will _____
(fill in with some of the actions that were named by the young people).

Blessed are these peacemakers,
for they will build pathways to peace
rather than weapons of violence.

Blessed are you, Lord,
the God of peace.

Bless this pathway;
may it lead us closer,
step by step,
to the peace that reigns in your kingdom.

We ask this through Christ our Lord.

All:	Amen.

CLOSING

Invite the young people to take someone else's brick home and pray their prayer during the coming week.

Give the young people a "Blessed Are the Peacemakers" button or 800-card.

Suggested songs include:

Lord, Bless Your People (Warner)
　　Voices as One Hymnal #59, CD 3 Track 7

On That Holy Mountain (Mattingly)
　　Voices as One Hymnal #68, CD 3 Track 14

We Are the Hope (Tate)
　　Voices as One Hymnal #97, CD 4 Track 17